BOOK OF STEVEN

Steven Petersen

Tellwell Talent

www.tellwell.ca

ISBN

978-1-77302-498-1 (Hardcover)

978-1-77302-496-7 (Paperback)

978-1-77302-497-4 (eBook)

Table of Contents

Introduction

My face is disintegrating.

Every time I look in my mirror I see living proof of infection. I am falling apart at the seams.

I've had lesions covering my forehead for over a year now. They creep down my chest and my arms. Imagine the worst acne you've ever had, then multiply it. Multiply the size of the zits by ten. Multiply the pain of them by one hundred. Multiply the rate of their rise and fall. Then imagine living with that face every day. It is as excruciating as it is humiliating. I wouldn't wish this on anyone.

Sometimes the pain lessens and I think, "It's not so bad." But then I look, and I see. My face is a mess. A complete wreck of a human face. It's bad. It's serious. Far beneath the skin, little shards work toward the surface until my body expels them, spewing them out in painful eruptions.

Disgusting.

Trust me. I know.

Every day, I come face to face with this. With myself. Every single time I look in the mirror and see what I'm dealing with, I get that sinking feeling in my gut again. Desperation. Despair.

The worst of it isn't even the pain. Or the mess. Or the humiliation. It's how this thing's shaken my confidence. I feel like I can't look at anyone in the face anymore. I can't face the world. Do you know how depressing it is, to see people flinch when they look at you? To know what they're thinking? *Junkie. Drug addict.* I see them look back at me sideways, furtively, trying not to stare. I see the thoughts start to play in their heads. *Loser. Get away from me. You should get that looked at. You should get help.*

Trust me, I'd love to get help. I really would. But that's the problem. No one can help me. Anyone who's in a position to try will just jump to conclusions. They won't hear a word of what I have to say, they'll disregard my lived experience, and they'll just decide that I'm crazy. Like, actually, certifiably nuts. I'll be locked away in an insane asylum before I can blink. As if that will do me any good. Treating the symptoms won't get me anywhere. It's the core of this disease I have to get at.

I've been lucky. At least I have some friends who believe me. And some family, too. People who have listened. People who have been beside me one hundred per cent through all of this. Who are still beside me. Their love and support is incredible. Their willingness to listen, to connect, to reach out—that is the greatest gift in the world. I am so, so thankful for them.

I've been lucky in another way, too—I have a business I can step away from. I don't have to show up for a day job, try to push through the pain and the emotional rollercoaster, nine to five, day in, day out. I don't have to fight for long-term disability that no one will even consider granting. Instead I've got an established store with an incredible staff who keep my business running. I am so indescribably grateful for all my employees. They have kept my store running through all of this. They have kept me afloat while I've been so down and out. I would never have had the chance to heal if it wasn't for them.

Each and every one of the people who have supported me has been a godsend. Even when I've let them down, even when I've been unavailable and struggling so much with my own pain and suffering, they have lent a helping hand or a listening ear. They have said, "Come on, Steve, you can do it." And you know what? I can. Because of them, I can.

Because of them, I am able to undertake the most important work of my life and share my story with you. Because of the support offered to me by a very few people, I can fulfil this mission: to tell you the truth of what has happened to me, to us, to all the life on this planet.

In these pages, I will tell you about this infestation that my body tries so painfully to reject. I will tell you the truth of it, the whole messy truth of it.

But in order for you to understand me, in order to grasp what this experience of living in my skin is like, I need to tell you about my life. About how I, too, was a young boy once, growing up with hopes and dreams, struggling to make the most of this sacred opportunity to live. I need to tell you about this because it's only when you see the whole picture of my life that you'll understand. It's the only way you can really know what I know. And once you know what I know, you'll be able to see how I figured out what was happening to me. How I have been able to grasp the truth, all the horrible ugly mess of it.

Here's my promise to you: Everything you read in these pages is my true lived experience. I'm sharing my life with you so you will be able to see what I see, know what I know, and understand what I believe.

I guarantee you that, at some points along the way, you will reject my words. You'll reject what I say out of hand. I know you will. I know that my story seems crazy. I won't blame you if you don't want to listen, or if, even when you listen, you don't believe me. My words are tough words. My story is really strange. My life is like something out of a science fiction movie, only stranger even than that. There will be places where you will not believe me. I know that.

What I'm asking is for you to remember that whatever you think you know—your values and assumptions about how the world is—these ideas are getting in your way. Your beliefs about what you think is true are interfering with your ability to hear me.

So stop. Leave that at the door. Whatever you think you know, set it aside. Listen to my story. Take it as a whole, on its own merits, as a full-meal deal. Allow yourself to ask, "What if?" Because hearing what I've been through might save you. Probably not. But it might. And even if it doesn't, I promise that if you hear me out, you will look at your life at least a little bit differently—with more love, with more empathy, with more willingness to live your life as if it matters. Because it does. Your life matters.

Mine does, too. Here's my story.

Chapter 1
Roots

In some respects, I was a saviour from the day I was born.

My coming into this world changed so much for my family. You see, I was the first one of us to be born on this continent. My parents were immigrants, and all my siblings were born in their home country of Denmark. I am the only one of us who was born Canadian.

Being the child of an immigrant leaves its mark. Things for immigrants are hard. Things that you and I take for granted were huge hurdles for them. Simple things become triumphs. That was especially true for my mom, Kirsten.

Because Kirsten was at home caring for four children, she didn't work out of the house, didn't get immersed in the community. She didn't have the same opportunities as my dad did to learn English. So even something as small as answering the door was a challenge. It might seem like no big deal to you, but my mother struggled to communicate the simplest things.

She told me once about this guy coming to the door early on, and because Mom didn't understand him he asked to speak with my dad. He kept saying, "Otto," and mimed talking with his hands. So Mom understood what he wanted. She said something like, "Otto, no home." Somehow the man managed to communicate that he could come back later, and he wanted to know when Dad would be there. But Mom didn't know the words for the time. So here's what she did—she went into the bedroom and came back with this little wind-up clock she had. She turned the dials until the hands showed eight o'clock. "Otto," she said, tapping the clock face, meaning, "Otto will be home at eight o' clock." It worked. But imagine having to communicate like that all the time. You really learn the power of words.

But I'm getting ahead of myself. Let me back up.

My story really starts with their story, with their decision to move to Canada. Without that choice, I'd be a very different person, assuming I'd even be here at all.

Kirsten Sorensen and Thorvald "Otto" Pedersen both grew up in Denmark, on the isle of Fyn. Both of them came from farm families with traditional backgrounds.

In Denmark, my dad was called by his given name of Thorvald, or by his nickname "Tay-Ho" (that's how you pronounce the letters *TH* in Danish). He was the youngest of eight children. When he was born, his father was fifty years old. If he were alive today, my grandfather would be 145!

Dad was an adventurer. I don't know if that's because he was the youngest—an anachronism in his family, almost—or if it's because Denmark got occupied by the Nazis when he was seventeen years old, or what. But he always loved to explore the world, to try things his way, find a way to figure things out, even if it was a bit unorthodox.

His boldness was practiced early. During the war, he was part of the resistance in Denmark for years; the Allies would drop parachutes with food and weapons and stuff into the coal pit where he worked, and he'd smuggle the arms out to other people on the island. He didn't get caught until April 28, 1945, a week before Denmark was liberated. He always said that the only reason he wasn't shot was that the Nazis knew the war was over, anyway. So they let him live. But that gave him a taste for life, I guess. He quit the coal pit, and went to Norway to apprentice as a machinist.

After that, he travelled in Europe—Switzerland and France mostly—and even went to Africa, getting out of Algeria when their civil war broke out. Only, he spent the last of this money on his ticket across the

Mediterranean to France, so getting back to Copenhagen (where he was living at the time) was an adventure in resourcefulness and relying on the kindness of strangers. He made it, though. He stayed in Sweden for a few years, working as a machinist. Then, in 1952, he went back home to Denmark, where he started his own trucking company, TH Trucking.

The trucking firm was pretty successful. He had a couple of trucks and a couple of busses, and he shipped farm commodities and people all over the island. During that time he met Kirsten Sorensen. After they'd known each other about a year, she moved into his house with her two children to work as his housekeeper. But turns out they were more than just employer/employee—they fell in love. On January 23, 1961, they got married.

Things turned sour for Dad in Denmark in 1960/1961. He lost his business. It's kind of a strange story. See, he didn't have enough money to buy a house, so he built his own instead. And he did a great job on it—it was big, beautiful and well made. That's the one he moved Kirsten into—he was very proud of that house and he loved that he had a family to fill it up with. Then he got his house assessed. It was worth so much money, he couldn't afford to pay the taxes on it! Eventually the government took his house and his business; his trucks were sold at auction.

That's when he knew he'd had enough of Denmark. If he wanted to get ahead, if he wanted to build a better future for his wife and kids, then he had to do something different. He decided to move to Canada. He had a brother there, Pete, who worked as a machinist in Calgary, Alberta. So a few months into his marriage, Otto headed to Canada to see what opportunities were available.

He made a good start in Canada. He got hired on at the machine shop where Pete worked right away. It was walking distance from Pete and Gerda's place—a good thing, as he didn't have a car—and he built a small circle for himself there.

Near the end of the year he went back home to Denmark to get the family. He was supposed to arrive in mid-December, but his ship was late, so he ended up arriving just in time to sit down to Christmas Eve dinner with his in-laws. That was a pretty magical day, not least because it was Christmas; it was the first time he got to meet his daughter, Helle.

My sister Helle had been born in October, while he was away, so he got to hold his first child for the first time on Christmas Eve.

My dad got to work sorting out the paperwork for the whole family to emigrate to Canada, and early in 1962 they left. In February, they boarded the Stavengerfjord, a passenger liner that ran from Oslo to New York City with a stop in the Danish capital of Copenhagen. Otto was thirty-eight years old; Kirsten was twenty-five. They had three small daughters in tow. My sister Helle was just four months old.

Kirsten was especially apprehensive about leaving the homeland. She'd spent her whole life on Fyn. Now she was sailing away from everything she knew, relying completely on her husband, with three daughters who were totally dependent on her. Canada held promise, true, but the challenges ahead would be extreme. She knew that. But she tackled it anyway. Because she wanted to give her children a better life. That's the kind of courage she had.

The voyage was terrible. It lasted ten days, and Kirsten was seasick the whole time. She literally spent the entire trip throwing up. When they arrived in New York, she weighed all of 110 pounds. Without my dad, my sisters would have had a really bad time of it. But he looked out for them all, sense of humour intact, maintaining morale, keeping them all looking forward to the adventure of their new lives ahead.

They landed in New York at the tail end of February. After passing through customs, they transferred to a train, and on March 1, 1962, the Pedersen family arrived at Fort Erie in Ontario. They became landed immigrants that day. The Canadian chapter of their lives had begun.

At that time, in the 1960s, car companies would pay folks to drive a car from Ontario out west in order to keep up with demand in the markets across the Prairies. So Otto was able to get the family across the country relatively cheaply. He managed to get a station wagon, and he folded down the seats in the back so the girls could sleep. They drove all day long, day after day, and they made the trek to his brother's place in just three days. Barely two weeks after leaving Denmark, the Pedersen family arrived in Calgary, Alberta.

For the first three weeks, the whole family lived with my uncle Pete and his wife Gerda. The day they arrived, there were already two other families staying there—Pete and Gerda were always helping new Danish families get started in Calgary. And things looked bleak at first. Dad was working at the machine shop again, but he'd borrowed four hundred dollars from Pete to bring his family over, and he insisted on paying it back. It looked as though everyone was going to be crammed into a few small bedrooms for a good long while.

But then Dad went out to the horse races, where he bet on the daily double, placing several bets front to back so he had his bases covered — and he won six hundred and eighty dollars. That was a lot of money back then; he was only making a dollar and eighty-five cents a day at the machine shop. So he paid Pete back, and then he found a small house for his family, just off the corner of Glenmore and McLeod Trails, right near Chinook Centre. It was a tiny little house — more of a shack, really — and they rented it for fifty dollars a month. But it was a space of their own. Kirsten and the girls moved in, trying to make it as homey as possible.

Meanwhile, Dad went to work every day, where he was becoming a new person. The machine shop is where he was first called by his Canadian name: Otto. See, none of his Canadian co-workers could say his real name properly; they pronounced it the way it looks in English, "Thorvald," instead of the way Danes say it, "Torwald." So he chose to go by his middle name, because everyone could say it right just by looking at it. And it wasn't just his first name that changed, either. In Denmark, Kirsten and Otto spelled their name "Pedersen," with a *d* in the middle. They'd say it the way an English speaker would say "Peterson." But in Canada, when people saw their last name spelled the Danish way, they would pronounce it "Pedderson." Otto never recognized himself as "Mr. Pedderson," so he changed the spelling, replacing the *d* with a *t*; that way, when his Canadian managers read his name out, they could pronounce it the way he expected to hear it. So my dad became "Mr. Petersen."

It wasn't only my father who had to adapt his name to his new home. The youngest of my sisters was called "Helle" in Danish, a two-syllable name — "hell-eh" — but in Calgary, everyone would drop the last *e*, pronouncing her name as "Hell." Not the nicest name for a baby girl! So Mom and Dad changed her name to Hellen; it was closer to their original intention. And it kept people from calling her Hell.

My mom never had to change her name. Not her last name nor her first name. Kirsten didn't have to face the same pronunciation obstacles that my dad did, because she wasn't working. On paper, though, it looked as if my parents had different last names.

Being called by a new name, changing the spelling of your last name—these things have an impact. I don't think it impacted Hellen very much, because she was so small. But it definitely affected Otto. He became a whole new person in some ways, took on a whole new identity. Maybe that's why he worked so hard to keep some of our other family traditions alive.

One of the biggest traditions in the Danish calendar is Christmas, which the Danes celebrate on Christmas Eve. That first year in the little shack by Glenmore Trail was where my family spent their first Christmas in Canada. Otto and Kirsten did their best to carry on the familiar traditions for their kids: almond riz, the marzipan pig, the Christmas tree in the middle of the room that everyone joined hands around, singing carols on Christmas Eve. And then, of course, the mysterious knock at the door, and when the kids went to open it, they found no-one—just a sack of presents! It was a real Danish Christmas in the Prairies, or as close to one as they could make it.

But in the background came the sounds of carousing from the bar at the corner of Glenmore and McLeod. My mom couldn't understand it: Why weren't those men home with their families? Why were they drinking Christmas night away? Didn't they have any culture? Otto tried to explain that that was their culture. All their friends were at the bar with them and many of them didn't have families. But it was a tough reminder for my parents, another example of this strange, outside world intruding on them, shaping them, changing them.

Anyway, despite the name changes and the language barriers and all the culture shock of the rough prairie life, my dad adapted pretty quick. He took things in stride; he did well for himself. In just over a year, he managed to save enough money to place a down payment on a house. In May of 1963, my parents bought a home of their own in Forest Lawn, in a community well-populated with other immigrants.

The move to Forest Lawn was a massive improvement, especially for Kristen. Being around other women from Germany and Denmark was a huge boost for her. Because she was at home all day with the children, she didn't get much opportunity to learn English, and so she couldn't have much of a conversation with anyone except Otto. She felt homesick and trapped. The new community made such a difference. And it wasn't only the neighbourhood—when they moved to Forest Lawn they also joined a church there: Emmanuel Lutheran Church.

The Lutheran Church is the national church of Denmark. So with the church came an immigrant congregation filled with families who understood the traditions of my parent's home, many of whom could speak Kirsten's native language. It was one of the only places Mom could go and feel comfortable. She was able to build a home away from home, to have real friends, to have others she could lean on. She was able to build relationships with people who could understand her—not only her words, but also what it was like to be so far from your family, to share things from home that she missed. It was a godsend, that church.

Funnily enough, they didn't go at first. It wasn't until my oldest sister encouraged it that they went at all. What happened was my sister had a friend from school who went to that church and who would go to the youth group, and she took my sister along. And pretty soon my sister was suggesting that the whole family ought to go to service on Sunday. So Mom took the kids and she loved it. She took the girls every Sunday. But Dad didn't want to go. Sunday was his one day off, and he didn't really want to spend it sitting in a pew. He didn't mind if Kirsten went and if she took the kids, but it wasn't first on his list.

But then one day Hellen said to him, "Dad, how come you don't come to church with us? Is it because you don't believe the things Pastor Grandburg is saying?" Well, after that, Dad came to church every single week. He'd be there in that pew, no matter what. He wasn't going to let his kids grow up not believing in God, even if it meant giving up his Sundays.

Another boost came for Kirsten when her brother Peter immigrated. That was in 1964, not long after they joined Emmanuel Lutheran. And then, in 1965, the family got a new, bigger house just around the corner from the old one. They were still in the same community near their friends and their church family, but they had more room to breathe.

The Petersens were making a life of it in Calgary, but still they felt unsettled. There were many ties back home still, many pulls. The new shift hadn't come easy, and the new language and customs seemed like they would be too much at times. Kirsten missed her family terribly, especially her father. Eventually, her father (my bestefar) got his papers in 1966 and came to visit on a one-way ticket, intending to stay as long as he could. He came in June and stayed until October. I think he probably would have stayed longer, but he got sick. Like, really sick—no one could figure out what was wrong with him. It didn't help that he couldn't communicate with the doctors because he hardly spoke any English. In any case, the family decided that the best thing for him was to return home to Denmark. Even if he couldn't get proper care there, at least he would feel confident that everything possible was being done for him. And that helped—he did get better after he flew back.

Despite his departure, though, life in Canada took a new turn for my family. Because my mom was pregnant again, with baby number four—who turned out to be me!

I was supposed to be born on my father's birthday: August 19th. But Otto's forty-fourth birthday came and went, and no baby arrived. Then, on September 5, 1967, on her thirty-first birthday, Kirsten went into labour. She walked Hellen to school for her first day of class, and went into labour on her way home. (Can you believe it? She didn't even get a single kid-free day!) Later that night, at 7:04 p.m. at Holy Cross Hospital in Calgary, I was born.

When Kirsten and Otto first held me, little tiny baby that I was, and looked at my wrinkled little face, they both thought instantly of Bent, Otto's father. They told me later that I looked just like my Bestefar—like a little, wizened old man.

And with my birth, my family had a brand new tie to their adopted homeland. My birth cemented my family's place in Canada. When I was born, my parents suddenly had real Canadian roots. I was a firm tie to this new place, and a firm bond in the family unit. I made the whole adventure worth it. When I was born, I made my family whole.

They had a good run of it. My parents stayed together, through the move out to the farm by Delburne when I was eight, and through the marriage of all their daughters. After we'd all grown up and gone, though, and they'd moved to Red Deer, there was nothing to hold them together anymore. They divorced in the early 2000s. Mom's still going strong; Dad lost a battle with lung cancer in 2010.

In its own way, his diagnosis was a blessing. I got to say goodbye to him. We got to have a good six months where we saw each other every single day. That time was such an incredible gift—getting to talk together, to be honest and open and just love each other. To thank God for all the time we'd had.

Mostly we didn't talk about anything big. It'd just be how everyone was doing, or what was going on at my store, or how the food was, or how my face was doing (every doctor I saw insisted it was stress-related acne). We reminisced a lot, talking about all the crazy cars I fixed up over the years. About how, when they took me to Denmark when I was five, I'd reply to the Danish kids in English, not realizing I wasn't speaking to them in the language they spoke to me. About the time I taught myself to swim in the Disneyland pool. We talked about anything and everything, sharing the little things, making every moment count. We were so happy that we could still be in the same room and talk to each other.

I got to thank him for being the best dad a kid could ever have. For all the sacrifices he and Mom made so I could have an amazing life. I really got the chance to step back and reflect on their incredible journey, on the amazing love they had, always, for my sisters and me. I mean, I am so blessed to have parents like that—with vision, with courage to uproot and start a new life, even when it was a really hard thing to do. Parents who knew what they had to do and did it, even when it was hard. I got to thank him, really thank him, for all of that.

Seriously, I can't even imagine how people cope when their loved ones just get snatched away. When they die in a car crash, or have a heart attack. I can't imagine not getting to say goodbye, or making sure that the last thing someone you love ever hears is, "I love you." That time with my dad at the end of his life was such an unbelievable gift. It made losing him bearable.

Otto passed away on December 26, 2010, at eighty-seven years old. It was hard. Grieving for someone you love is brutal. But it was joyful, too. My dad had lived a really full life, an amazing life. He wasn't ready to go—he thought he was too young to die because everyone in his family lived into their nineties—but at least now he doesn't suffer anymore.

One of the most beautiful things, for me, came out after the funeral. A couple who were both friends of my dad's took me aside and said they wanted to share something. "You know, Steven," they said, "we asked your dad what was the one thing in his life that he was most proud of, and you know what he said? You. In his mind, you were the one thing in all his life that made your dad the most proud."

Well, that broke me. I cried like a baby. Do you know what it's like to hear that about yourself? What it's like to know that your father loved you—that he really, genuinely cared about you, above everything else in this life? It's pretty incredible.

Dad's words really brought home to me that I was a special force in my parents' lives. And I had this strong feeling that I needed to make the most of it. They had given up so much, risked so much, just so they could create a better future for their kids. And I owed it to them to build on that.

I was already making good on that in some ways—I'd built up my eyewear business to be pretty successful by that point. But I wasn't fulfilling everything within me. I knew that, somehow. I was forty-five years old and I still had no idea what the real purpose of my life was.

That ate at me. It bothered me a lot. I mean, it's one thing to have a wonderful family and be financially successful. It's another to know you're giving everything of yourself to the world, living out whatever greatness is in you.

I knew, somehow, somewhere inside, that I wasn't doing that. I wasn't giving it my all. Ever since I was a young boy, growing up in the church in Calgary, I just had this sense that I was put on the earth for a special purpose. But I'd never really found what that was. I mean, I'd always been searching. But I hadn't found it. And I was more aware than ever that my time on this earth was slipping by, and slipping by fast.

After Dad died, I was determined to find my destiny. Knowing my purpose in life became a huge focus for me. I started digging inside myself, questioning the world, more fully than I ever had before. But all the while, my face kept getting worse and worse. The acne-like things became more and more persistent. They lasted longer. They were more painful.

Some part of me really resented it. Here I was, finally determined to find my real meaning, and I hated being slowed down by this mess that was taking over my time and attention. I went to doctors, even took IV vitamin injections on a regular basis to try and boost my overall health. I wanted to be bigger, stronger, more fit. I wanted to be healthier. But most of all I wanted to beat whatever was burrowing under my skin.

None of it did any good, really. It just got slowly worse, up until the spring of 2015. Then whatever was under my skin erupted, and I hit my breaking point. How was I supposed to live out my life to the absolute fullest when I could barely face myself in the mirror?

Chapter 2
Independence

It takes a lot to break me. I'm a pretty resilient guy. I've been through a lot. I've done a fair amount in my time. Whatever I wanted to pursue, I've done it: gold panning in northern B.C., racecar driving, making a television show. All that on top of all my optical jobs! But when I realized I couldn't look myself in the eye anymore, well, that was pretty tough to take. I mean, if I can't stand to look at me, how can anyone else? And I knew then that something had to change. Something needed sorting out. And it was up to me to make that happen.

I've always been like that, too. I remember this one time—I think I was about five—I needed to learn how to tie my shoes so I could go to kindergarten. My parents showed me how to do it, but I had real trouble making the laces do what they were supposed to do. I tried and I tried, but I couldn't do it, and I was getting frustrated, and everyone was laughing at me. Well, maybe it was funny to them, but it wasn't funny to me. So I went and shut myself in my room and stayed in there until I could finally do it. And then I came out and declared that I could do it. I'd needed time and space to figure it out on my own.

Growing up, that attitude was normal in my family. The expectation was that if something went wrong, you were the one who had to figure out a way to make it right. You didn't go looking to anyone else. You looked to yourself first. You relied on your own hands and your own brain to make your way in the world. I mean look at my parents. Danish immigrants, came here with nothing—came here in debt—and they became landowners, property owners, business owners. They built a lot out of nothing.

That attitude was reinforced after we moved out to our farm. That was when I was eight years old. My family moved from Calgary to a little town near Red Deer called Delburne. A friend of Dad's was opening a foundry there, and he wanted Otto for his machinist. So my parents bought some land just outside of the town—finally, a farm of their own.

My parents were pretty happy to be back in the country. They were both from farm families, rural families. My dad's family raised eight kids on eight acres, and all of a sudden he had a whole quarter section—one hundred and sixty acres of land to call his own. Their Canadian dream came true.

Anyway, they moved to the farm with Hellen and me. My other two sisters were grown up by then and had families of their own back in Calgary.

Moving to the farm brought a whole new phase of my life. In the city, I had a lot of free time to do my own thing, to play with my friends and stuff. Out in the country, life was very different. I had responsibilities. I had chores I needed to do every day. Feeding the chickens in the morning. Letting the stock out when I got home. All kinds of things. Farms are a lot of work. Everyone needs to contribute, or things don't get done.

That was a big change. I mean, yeah, in the city I'd had my own bit of garden in the backyard. We all did. But the family didn't depend on it for anything; if I forgot to water it, and my plants died, it didn't have a material impact. Out at the farm things were different. If I didn't do my chores, it mattered. It mattered a lot.

Because both my parents were working, Hellen and I had to be self-accountable every day. Our parents wouldn't be home when we got home. We had to choose to do our chores ourselves. And we did.

If I'm being honest, we were mostly motivated by getting things done in time for our favourite TV shows. That was always a fight, I tell you. She wanted to watch her soap opera, and I wanted to watch cartoons.

Guess who won that every day? But at least with the chores I had something to bargain with. Every now and again I could convince her that I'd do her round of dishes or something and we'd watch cartoons. Not often. But I remember several times I was able to convince her.

It wasn't just chores I had to look after, either. Another thing I had to be responsible for was getting out to the school bus every day. I didn't walk to school anymore. Now I had to be out at the end of our driveway every day, ready for when the bus went past, or I'd miss it. Every day, rain or snow or shine. Even in minus-thirty-degree weather I had to be out there. And if I wasn't, then there would be a phone call to Mom at work in town to see if she could come get me. Sometimes she would. Mostly she'd make me walk, or ride my bike. After all, it was up to me to be on time for that bus, and if I had to walk the few miles into town, well, that'd teach me to not be late the next morning.

I remember another thing about accountability. At school, I kept hearing my friends talk about how they'd get paid for their report cards: twenty dollars for an A, maybe, ten dollars for a B, stuff like that. Well, I thought that sounded like a great idea. I brought that up with my dad one day, when he came to pick me up in his truck. I suggested that maybe I should be getting paid for my grades, too. I'll never forget the look he gave me. Then he just turned to the road, put the truck into gear, and said, "If I have to pay you to do your best, we've got a serious problem." And that was the end of that conversation. Let me tell you, I never forgot it.

Growing up in my family that demanded responsibility had its good points, too. It meant that I got to be responsible for myself. As I got older, that translated into more and more independence. As long as I went to school and took care of my chores at home, I could spend the rest of my time how I liked. Usually that meant heading over to a friend's house on my bike.

My best friends were my nearest neighbours; that's how things work in the country. Not always, but pretty often. You're friends with the people around you. You have to be; you rely on each other so much out there. Mike and Darren were the guys I knew the best. When we first moved out there, I'd have to walk to their place, or my parents would drop me off. After I got a bike, though, that was it—I'd be off on my own all the time.

Man, that bike was my ticket to freedom when I first got it. I was eleven years old, and I had a crappy old one. But I had my eye on a really nice one, a souped-up one, a superbike! A Raleigh sport bike. Boy, did I want it bad. That bike was like my true love. I saved up one hundred and eighty dollars for it, collecting copper wire for the scrap metal guys, saving all my money from helping Dad at the foundry, and I did it. I bought myself that bike. It was glorious.

Once I had it, though, I wasn't satisfied for long. Pretty soon I wanted a dirt bike. If a bike was fun, a dirt bike was ten times as much fun. Loud and fast and cool—I wanted a dirt bike so bad. Dad helped me buy my first one. He was magnificent at finding deals. I only had a little bit of money, but we got a little used bike from a farm a few miles away for dirt cheap. I really rode that bike into the ground. I rode it till it broke down, and even my dad, a crack mechanic, couldn't make it start up again. So eventually we got a bigger one, a Kawasaki KX 80—it had way too much power for me, and Dad warned me not to race. I pushed it anyway. Of course. Pushed too far and popped the clutch, flipped over backwards and broke the fender. Dad wasn't too pleased about that.

Bikes led to cars, of course. As soon as I could, I got my learner's licence. I had to take the test twice—I failed the first time. But I passed it on the second try. And then there was no stopping me. Dad would let me drive everywhere. Once I was sixteen and got my full licence, Dad gave me the old field truck to drive, a 1970 Ford half-ton, three-on-the-tree, two-hundred-and-forty horse power, six-cylinder engine. Field trucks are always in rough shape; they do all the hard jobs on the farm, so they're beat up and battered and the suspension is shot, and the engine chokes. But I didn't care. A truck is a truck at sixteen, and I knew enough by then to know I could make it my own.

Well, I took that old truck down to my brother-in-law's place, and together we restored that beauty. Dad and I rebuilt the whole engine. I did all the body work myself—made a ton of mistakes but I learned a lot, too—and we painted it candy apple red, put in a fancy stereo and some fuzzy dice on the mirror. That old hunk of junk looked amazing by the time we were done with it. It was such a treat.

Driving opened up a whole new world of fun. I remember this one time in the middle of winter, it was on a Sunday, I'm pretty sure, because all the shops were closed and there was nobody around. Well, very few people anyway. I was hanging out with some friends, and we decided it would be a lot of fun to ski from the fenders of my car. So we got ourselves some mini-skis, and a couple of long ropes, just like you would if you were waterskiing. And then we'd fly down the streets, those guys hanging on for dear life behind the car. At the end of Main Street there was this big parking lot that looked onto a field, and I'd turn the car hard, and they'd go whipping out across the field--wheeee! Man, was that a good time. We got a few complaints about that one—us whooping and hollering and carrying on down Main Street, whipping along on those ropes. Could've caused a lot of damage. Our parents heard about it, and made us apologize. So it hurt our pride. But not much else, luckily. A few bumps and scrapes—that was all.

In the summer time, though, fishing was the way to go. I'd go out fishing with my friends quite a bit. My friend Darren's dad taught me how to fish. Otto had no experience as a sportsman, couldn't fish to save his life. So Darren's dad taught me. I'd go down to the river with them maybe once a week, and pretty soon I caught my biggest fish. Man, was I proud! I came home grinning ear to ear and made Mom take a picture— me all scrawny and dwarfed by my hat and holding up this pike, half the size of me, with the biggest, goofiest grin on my face.

That was part of a long, proud tradition. Some days, when the evenings were so long, we'd head down to the river, usually with Mike, and we'd hang out and toss out our lines. Honestly, after a while it didn't matter if we caught anything or not. Just being out there, being alive, hearing the water run, nowhere to be and nothing to do—that was the best feeling in the world. The absolute best.

I didn't do a lot in the way of extra-curricular activities. I didn't really get the whole organized-sport thing. I was athletic enough, but I hated the idea of a coach telling each person what to do, having really specific jobs, and then getting told you let the team down even if you did your job perfectly. The coaches for the teams never really seemed to get the idea of team spirit, of a goal and a feeling that can unite a group of people if they believe in it. Instead they got super-detailed, trying to manage and control everything. I hated that.

The one thing I did do was Air Cadets. There was a squadron in Stettler, and I'd go with a bunch of friends from school. I started Air Cadets when I was in grade eight. We would make the drive up to Stettler once a week. My uncle Peter, Mom's brother, had been in the military in Denmark, and he was the person who led our Air Cadet squadron. A bunch of us kids from the area would meet down at the old arcade, load onto a bus, and Dad would drive us up to Stettler where we'd meet everyone else. There were about twelve of us in all, at first. Mostly guys, but a couple girls.

I talked a bunch of my friends from school into coming, partly because I loved it and thought they would too if they gave it a try. It was something so different and we got to learn about planes, go on camp outs, and have dances and stuff. But I also wanted them to join because it was cheaper that way. We had to rent the bus and pay for gas, and the more people we had, the cheaper it was for everyone.

I loved Air Cadets. Something about how it was all set up just worked for me. Maybe it was the whole idea of everyone working toward a single goal, all in it together, all motivated by a vision and a purpose. Or maybe it was the whole thing of being self-accountable. I mean, I knew exactly what the troop leader would be looking for each week, and I'd black my boots really carefully and press my shirt, and I'd be all ready to go for inspection.

I excelled at Air Cadets. I got promoted in rank faster than anyone else. I made corporal in a couple of months, and then sergeant not quite a year after that. By the time I'd made sergeant, some of the kids I'd started with hadn't even made corporal yet, even though it was obvious what we needed to do each week. I guess they just didn't see that.

Anyway, being in Air Cadets was a lot of fun, and provided me with some amazing opportunities. We'd do our flight training and simulations and stuff over at the air force base at Penhold (back before it became the Red Deer Regional Airport). We all got to go flying, which was a pretty cool opportunity. And I also got the chance to go on a couple of leadership training camps. One was way up in the Yukon. We spent a week in classes and then a week travelling down the river, whitewater rafting and stuff, putting into practice what we'd learned. I think I was fifteen or sixteen when I got to do that, so it was pretty incredible. One other guy from the Stettler squadron went with me—actually, he was one of the Delburne crew—but it was just the two of us.

I think part of the reason I did so well at Air Cadets is that it was an extension of the things I learned at home: Look out for what you're responsible for, pitch in and work toward a bigger goal. It just made sense to me. I loved it.

Anyway, I stayed in Air Cadets through high school, until it dissolved when I was in grade eleven. There just weren't enough new recruits, so there weren't enough of us to keep the squadron going after a while. That was tough. Especially because going to school just kept getting harder and harder for me to take.

After a while, I just didn't get the point of school anymore. So much of what we had to learn made no sense to me. I couldn't see any reason why I'd need to know any of it. And the teachers all treated you like some kid, trying to control you, rein you in. By grade ten I was already rebelling. I dyed my hair blue. After a while I got my ear pierced and started smoking. By the time grade twelve hit and Air Cadets was done, I couldn't make myself care anymore. I'd spend more time in the smoking room than in class. (They had a smoking room in our high school back in the 1980s, if you can believe it. It was so thick with smoke the air was blue in there. The walls just dripped nicotine. But it was such a refuge—the coolest place in school to hang out, if you could stomach it.)

That whole year was tough. I didn't pass my grade twelve math. Didn't get my fifty per cent. I don't get why there's this arbitrary cut off—why if you know forty-eight per cent of the material, you don't get any credit, but if you get fifty per cent of the material, then you get all the credit. It seems really stupid; there should be a better system than that. Anyway, I didn't pass math. And that meant I didn't have enough courses to graduate, not unless I stuck around for a whole other year and did math again the next fall.

Well, I wasn't having any of that. No way. I decided that winter that I was going to quit. I wasn't interested in playing their games anymore, jumping through anybody's hoops, saying "Yes, sir, this is the answer, sir," just so I could get some marks and some stupid piece of paper. So I dropped out of high school. I wanted to get a real education instead. I wanted to learn about how the world really ticks.

In my family, if you weren't going to school, you were expected to work. You were expected to contribute to the household, and all of its work and expenses. So there I was, seventeen years old in the spring of '85, looking for a job as a high school dropout—things aren't so clear, you know? It's hard.

I worked for a few months at a computer store, selling these computer accounting packages. But it didn't really suit me, wasn't my thing. Computers have never really been my thing. Then I got a job with a company called Interstate Engineering Corporation. It sounds fancy and all that, but what it really was was a vacuum company. And I was a vacuum salesman—selling vacuums in people's homes. Not really what you want to leave high school for, but there I was. At least it was a job. A paying gig.

It's crazy when you think about it—this seventeen-year-old kid sitting down in stranger's front rooms, selling them vacuums. I did pretty well, though. I like people. And, I mean, the vacuum we were selling was a pretty cool little gadget. It worked great. So I'd go in there, and I'd do a basic little demo, show them how it worked, all the little tricks it could do. People would be sitting with jaws dropped, mouths hanging open— that's how cool that vacuum was. It was such a good machine that it was pretty easy to sell. But think about it. Seventeen years old, sitting down on a stranger's front couch, and having to sell. It's a pretty bold endeavour for a young person. Let me tell you, all those leadership courses I took in Air Cadets paid off big time. Big time.

It was quite the job! Great for me, really, in the end. I got to learn how the real world works. How people work, what makes them tick. What makes them buy things, part with their hard-earned cash. Plus I learned how to talk to people. I could talk to anyone after that job. I got to see how a whole lot of different people lived, see different communities and cultures, and find a way to talk to them, anyway. We'd travel all over Alberta, as far south as Medicine Hat and all the way up to Grand Prairie, selling vacuums. So I got to meet a lot of cool folks.

I did pretty well at it, too. Out of every ten homes, I'd sell maybe four vacuums. Some weeks would be more, some a little less. But I didn't have too many weeks in a row where I'd make just a few sales. Mostly I did pretty well; I was pretty consistent. But there was this one guy in the company, let's call him Warren. Man, could that guy sell. It seemed like out of every ten houses he'd visit, he'd sell nine vacuums. People just couldn't say no to him.

We couldn't either. Every road trip, we'd have poker games, and Warren, he'd clean us all out, every time. Every time! I stopped playing after a few tries. I like to keep some of my pay cheque, thanks. But some of the other guys, they'd lose every time, week in, week out. He'd talk them into playing every week, and then he'd take their money. Eventually I figured he had to have a secret, some trick that made him so good. So I watched him. I asked him about it. And I learned two things.

First of all—and this is important—if people are even talking to you, they're in the market. They're interested in buying what you're selling. If they come into your store, or let you into their home, they're already thinking "I want this thing," or "I think I could use this."

Second, and most important, selling is all about the edges. With each client, you've got to find the edges, and you've got to use them. You do that, and you almost don't even have to work at all.

Here's how it works: You give your spiel then you sit back and you listen. You wait for your clients to give you an edge. And when they do, you hop on it. You hop on that edge, and you use it. If you do that, your clients will sell the product to themselves. You don't even have to do anything at all.

Let me give you an example. Say I'm sitting in Dave and Maggie's front room. I give my little demonstration with the vacuum, and then I sit back, and I wait. I listen. And maybe Dave says to Maggie, "So, Maggie, what do you think?" And that's an edge. So I hop on it. I might say something like, "You know, before you answer that, Maggie, can I just say—I do this a lot. I spend a lot of time in people's homes, talking about vacuums. And it sure doesn't happen often when a husband turns to his wife and says 'What do you think?' I mean, Dave–thanks. You get that she's going to be using this, too. Maybe more than you. I love that you respect that."

I know that speech doesn't seem like a lot. It doesn't seem that profound. It might not even seem relevant. But see what I've done? I've made Maggie feel special for having a husband who cares. I've made Dave feel special for looking out for his wife, for his consideration of her.

Now they're both in a good mood. They're in a position to think positively of this little vacuum and what it represents to them. And suddenly, it's a reminder of these really nice values they each have for each other. Now Dave wants to buy this little vacuum for Maggie, to show her that he really does value her and look out for her. Of course, there's a long way to go from there. But it's a start. They can talk each other into it now, because the door's open.

That's just one small example, and a pretty subtle one. Sometimes edges are more obvious. Like, I'd take my vacuum into a mechanic's house, or into a place where the guy likes to tinker with gadgets. Well, then, that's easy. We can get all nerdy over the crazy mechanical workings of this little beauty of a vacuum, and he'll see no reason not to buy it.

Anyway, learning about the edges was one of the best things I took away from the vacuum company. After I learned that, I did much better than before. I still wasn't flying as high as Warren, selling nine out of ten vacuums. But I'd be selling six or seven out of ten most of the time.

I worked for Interstate Engineering Corporation for a few years. I was based out of Red Deer for a long time, and then I moved up to Edmonton. That was pretty exciting, living in the big city and running their operation up there. I had fun with that for a while. But by the time I transferred down to Calgary to start up a branch there, I was starting to get bored of it. Once you learn the ropes, learn the product, and have been in enough homes, it all starts to look the same. And I was starting to care more about using people's edges than whether or not they really needed the vacuum. And once you do that, things can get ugly fast. So I decided it was time to close that chapter of my life and move on.

But it taught me something really valuable, that job. It taught me about people, and about selling, sure. And those things serve me well even now in my business. But it taught me something else, something much more important—that no matter what environment I found myself in, and no matter what challenges I faced, I could see my way to making it work for me. If I paid attention and listened and was open to learning, I could turn any tricky situation into gold. I just have to remember that seventeen-year-old kid, sitting on a stranger's sofa, pitching his first sale, and I remember: I can do it.

That's kept me going through a lot of tough times. And it keeps me going now, with whatever this ugliness is in my skin. I know that whatever happens, I can solve this problem. I will beat this thing festering inside me, bubbling in my skin. I will find a way to fix it, to make it right, even when it feels so daunting, so overwhelming, so impossibly huge that I think—why me? Why am I the person who has to face this mess?

Chapter 3
Vision

Vision has been a part of my life for a long time. And I mean that in more ways than one. On a literal level, I'm in the eyewear business, and I have been for a while. I've been helping people with eyeglasses for over twenty-five years. On a more spiritual level, I've always been invested in learning to see beyond the physical. Maybe that comes from growing up in a church. But I've always been drawn to it.

Sometimes I'll joke with my customers. Sometimes, they'll say, "What do you think? Do I see okay?" and I'll say, "Well, maybe in one way you don't, but in another way—yeah, you see pretty good." When you spend your whole life paying attention to more than just the surface layer of things, you can tell pretty quickly whether people are seeing beyond the end of their own nose.

In so many ways, it's no surprise I chose a visionary trade. Vision really matters to me. Seeing clearly matters, on every level. If you can't see clearly, how can you tell where you're going? How can you figure anything out?

When I first started in the eyewear industry, I had no idea I was going to make it my life. I just needed a job. I was working in an optical store in the mall in Red Deer, maybe twenty years old, just being the sales guy on the floor. I hardly knew a thing about glasses beyond what I'd learned when I got my first pair at thirteen, but I had to try and sell them.

It didn't take me long to learn that selling glasses was easy. People wanted them. They came into the store expressly to look for them. All I had to do was help them find the right pair. It was simple and it was fun, and I could see it made a real difference in their lives. Clear sight is such a gift. It gives people confidence. It lets the world come to them without a fight. And the frames you put on your face shape the way you show yourself to the world. I realized that selling people glasses made me feel as if I was really helping them, as if I was doing something that mattered, something that made their lives better. I loved that.

It was a big part of how I was raised—you don't just live for you. You live a life that helps the people around you, too. I mean, look at a rural life, a farm life—everyone pitches in and helps everyone else. But it wasn't just that. I think part of that helping ethic came from growing up in a church.

Because the church was my mom's safe environment, especially in Calgary, I spent a lot of time there as a kid. Mom would be there almost every day, helping out with lunches for a funeral, or prepping for youth group, or fundraising for whichever event or mission trip was happening. So I spent a lot of time running around in the church while she was helping out.

Right from the beginning, I was raised the old fashioned way—in the church, surrounded by loving family, a loving community. It was a Danish tradition, part of the Danish fabric of life. Over in Denmark, all the records are kept in the church: births, baptisms, marriages, deaths, you name it. The church was the heart of the community. My parents approached their Canadian lives like that, too. I was baptized at that Emmanuel Lutheran Church on October 8, 1967, with my dad's brother Pete and his wife Gerda Petersen as my godparents. I was truly a child raised by a village. I loved that church. I remember it really well.

Like any community, though, a church needs a leader. And we had an amazing one: Pastor Grandburg. He was a living example of how vision and inspiration and commitment can shape a whole community. Boy, was he a leader! In the pulpit, he could command the whole room. He'd have everyone hanging on his words. And if you were drifting off, or thinking something didn't apply to you, he'd know. And he'd look straight at you from up there. All he had to do was look at you, and you'd snap to. You'd pay attention all right, and you'd know you'd better have a think and listen carefully to the words coming out of his mouth. He burned right to the heart of his congregation when he was in the pulpit.

But when you got to talk to him person to person, he was very gentle, very sincere. He talked to you like a human being, like a person who mattered. He saw God in all of his congregation, so they saw God in him. And he dedicated himself to the one love of his life: Christ.

Growing up in a church community with a leader like that was such an opportunity. It taught me about things that are bigger than myself. It taught me how important it was to look beyond myself, to help other people out there in the world. I think I always looked for that, even though I didn't know it. It's part of why I loved Air Cadets so much; that kind of leadership mattered.

Anyway, when I found myself working in that first eyewear store in Red Deer, and I saw how much of an impact a simple thing like glasses had on people, I thought, I want to pursue this. I want to help people correct their vision. So I signed up to do my optician's diploma.

It wasn't an easy path, though. Not for me, anyway. My boss at the optical store agreed to mentor me. Only, he didn't really mean it. Whenever I had questions and would go to him for help or answers or whatever, he'd put me off. Act as if I wasn't there or go find something else to do. Or else he'd promise to tell me about it later and then deliberately "forget." It's as if he did everything he could not to help me. As if he thought that if I took this course I'd be better than him, or something.

Needless to say, I failed. That took the wind out of my sails for a while. But it didn't matter in the long run. I kept working at optical stores, working towards my diploma. I even ended up moving to Edmonton for a while, working in a store there. I stayed with my aunt and uncle until I got a place. Eventually I ended up getting transferred to the Millwoods branch, which closed down not long after I started there. But that was okay. I had a good taste of the optical world by then, and I liked it a lot.

I still hadn't made a pair of glasses, though. And I needed work, so I applied for a job up in northern B.C. at a lab that makes glasses. The owner flew me up for an interview; boy, did I bullshit my way through that one! Said I'd cut lenses a bunch of times, and I was sure I could do it on his machine, too, if he'd be sure and show me how it worked.

Well, he took me on. He showed me how to cut lenses, and I paid real close attention while he showed me the first couple pairs. Because I was learning as I went, it was all new to me, even though I acted as if it wasn't. And I got through the first few pairs on my own okay. Pretty soon I was doing it real well—I got so I was making fifty pairs of glasses a day after a couple of weeks.

The machine he had was pretty old-school. You had to cut a plastic piece first, and then use that as a template to cut your lenses with, kind of like tracing it in the machine. Most of the lenses were still glass then. Now they're mostly plastic. And now you just program the computer in the machine, and it does the figuring for you. But when I learned, it was by hand, the old-fashioned way.

He was the best boss I ever had, that guy. Believed in rewarding hard work. Believed in giving people chances. He was a real helper. Working with him was a great opportunity. He even flew me back to Edmonton so I could finish my optician's diploma. Amazing, eh? I think he could tell that I cared. That I wasn't just in it for the money. That I wanted to help people, too.

I didn't stay up north for too long after I finished my diploma, though. Things ended badly up there because of an idiot acquaintance of mine, and I got out of the eyewear business for a bit. I moved back home to the farm and started in workwear. I got a job at a workwear store in Red Deer, and then I started up a workwear business in Caroline. But that didn't pan out, so I got back into optical. I worked for another optical store in Red Deer for a while, and then transferred down to Calgary so I could take my contact lens diploma. And from there I moved out to Nelson, B.C., to take on my first job as an eyewear store manager.

Nelson was an awesome experience. For the first time, I was responsible for running the whole store. It was a big step up in responsibility, but I was ready for it. I put all my sales experience to good use, and I built that business up a lot; by the time I left I had doubled the revenue there several times over. It was the first time I saw that I wasn't the person benefitting from my own hard work, though. I was lining someone else's pocket. And yeah, my hourly wage went up a few bucks an hour over the years, but it was nowhere near what I was bringing in for the owner.

I didn't really care too much, then. I was still just soaking in the joy of being alive. Nelson was such an experience. What a place to be an independent adult. Life really is different out in B.C. Just real laid back. Everyone smoking pot and singing songs around the fire. I felt so alive out there. The job was just one piece of a full and easy life.

Living in Nelson really changed me, and it wasn't just because of the lifestyle, or the job. I grew spiritually there, too. I started to tap into this broadened vision of the world.

One of the things I learned in Nelson was this whole idea that the world is answering your questions all the time; you just have to learn to pay attention. You have to look at how all the little pieces are part of a much bigger picture. Everything around you that's happening right now can reveal something about you and your life.

One of my friends out there—let's call him Mark—showed me an ancient Chinese divining system called the I Ching. The I Ching is a way of seeing what the future holds. There's a whole art and method and ritual to it that I don't need to go into (you can check out the resources at the back of the book if you want to learn about it—it's pretty cool). But basically what you do is observe the world around you, and you meditate on it, and match up what you see with the things you're thinking about and the questions you have about life.

The I Ching taught me that life is always offering you clues, giving you answers to questions. Sometimes, it's trying to answer the questions you didn't even know you had. But you have to be paying attention in order to see it. And it takes a long time to learn to keep your eyes open as you walk through life every day. It's a process. It's kind of like praying. You try to formulate your questions when you talk to God, but then you go through your day living and observing and paying attention to the world. And sometimes what you see in the world is an answer to your prayers. And sometimes what you see in the world helps you refine your questions.

It's as if life is always trying to talk to you and get your attention. And I learned that it was up to me to pay attention, to listen to what I was being told. That's how you live rightly, in my book. You pay attention—you listen, you learn, and you try your best to be a good human.

I've put that into practice over the years. I've tried to ask questions and watch for signs and integrate how I see things into whatever the world is trying to tell me. I did that pretty well in Regina, and I learned new ways of doing years later when I was working in Wetaskiwin.

Wetaskiwin is out by Maskwacis, which is a First Nation community in Central Alberta. While I was working for a guy there, I learned to read people's totems. Reading people's totems is kind of like the I Ching, only more about people and how they are, and less about the moment or the future.

Anyway, one of the things you develop when you listen to the world all the time is confidence. A willingness to just go for things. This trust that it'll all work out, that there's a divine plan. While I was there in Wetaskiwin, working for someone else in yet another eyewear store, managing it, building this guy's store and bringing in lots of revenue, I realized it was really starting to rankle me, working for someone else. And that's how I came to start my eyewear business. Because I was paying attention to the big picture of my life, listening to myself and the world, I realized that working hard for a wage while my work was lining someone else's pockets just wasn't working for me anymore. It was time to change.

That isn't to say I don't value work. Or that I thought I should be making more money. Nothing like that. One thing I have always cared about—maybe because my dad really made me learn it—is that you have to work for what you get. I always knew my whole life that things weren't going to be handed to me. That never worried me. I figured I'd manage to make my way. I kept working hard, banging my head against a brick wall sometimes, but I'd get things done. The thing is, working hard for a wage will only get you so far. I looked around me and I realized that it was time to go into business for myself.

After all the stores I'd run—first in Nelson, and then in Regina, Camrose, and Wetaskiwin—I knew everything I needed to know about the optical industry. And not just the selling side, either—the industry as a whole. By the time I landed in Wetaskiwin, I'd already spent years and years building up knowledge about how the industry worked. Being an optician. Cutting lenses. Ordering coatings and tints on lenses. Repairing frames. Fitting frames. The works.

And running a successful business isn't just about the trade. It's about dealing with people. Understanding them. As a business owner, you've got to manage customers. You've got to manage your staff, and your space. But I knew how to do all that. I was doing all that, anyway, only my efforts were going to benefit someone else. I was already running the place. Now I wanted to run *my* place.

One of the most important things I knew was that location matters. A lot. So when I was working in Wetaskiwin—the last place I worked for someone else—I started keeping an eye out for a good location in Red Deer.

Why Red Deer? I guess because Red Deer's the hub of Central Alberta. People want to be there. Plus it was close to my family—my parents had sold the farm and moved into town by then, and I was ready to spend some more time with them. After all the help they'd given me over the years, I wanted to be able to turn around and help them out when they needed it. And in a way, going back to Red Deer was going full circle. Red Deer was the starting place for my optical journey, where I'd first had the idea that maybe being an optician was the path for me. Now I could bring all my knowledge, all my skills, back with me and show the world what I was capable of.

Once I decided on Red Deer, I started watching for a good location, and it wasn't too long before one came up between the two sides of town, with Main Street flowing past on either side. I figured that would be a bullseye. Everyone in town could get there easily. And everyone in town would see the signs, whichever way they travelled. So when a bay came up in the little mall there, I jumped on it.

I put in an offer to lease the bay, and then I set to work putting together my finances. I scraped and borrowed, begged and stole, from everyone I knew, but I only managed to get together about fifteen thousand dollars. Obviously, I was going to need more than that. Lucky for me, there were small business loans available then. I was eligible for a fifty thousand dollar loan and I figured that would be enough. I sat down, and I figured out what equipment I would need and figured I could get started on fifty thousand dollars.

That loan was a lifesaver—don't get me wrong. But it was also a night-mare. I had to keep track of literally every single penny. There was only one bank that would administer a loan like that to me, and they needed every single cent accounted for. So I had to have a perfect, one hundred per cent complete paper trail. Nothing missing. Every time I wanted money I'd need an invoice, then go to the bank, get the money, go back with a receipt—it was crazy.

But I did it. I got a whole bunch of my basic equipment second-hand—it's amazing what you can get cheap when you look for it. I had to get some of it shipped in, but that was okay. I was getting such a good deal it was still worth it. And I ordered a stock of frames on great terms; I'd have a chance to sell them before I had to pay for them. So I could see my way toward making it work.

The most difficult thing was actually the renovations. Setting up the store itself. I got a whole bunch of different guys in, got quotes, and they all came in at at least fifty thousand. That was my whole loan! There was no way I could spend that on getting the place set up. That was never going to happen. How could I pay for anything else? Just like it always is—guys wanting easy money and not wanting to do the work. It's shame-ful, man. And they get away with it!

But then I found an amazing guy—let's call him Danny. Danny gave me a quote that was a fraction of the fee that the other guys charged. He was an old-fashioned, hard-working type—not afraid of a little elbow grease. Anyway, he set up that place for me, and it turned out just the way I wanted. He spent so many hours on it and even brought in his wife to help him, but he got it all done, and he got it done on time. Sure, it might not have had quite the polish that some of those other guys might've given it, but then who knows? And anyway, it was plenty good enough to suit me.

I set it up the way it is—with a fountain in the front and a couch and magazines—because I wanted it to feel as if you were coming into some-one's home instead of walking into a showroom. It's intimidating when the first thing you walk into is a showroom, with all its bright lights and so many options staring down at you from the walls. That's no good. It shuts people down before they even start shopping. No, my place was going to be different. You were going to be treated like family, and you'd feel like family. Customer service is and always has been my number one priority.

After all these years in the industry there isn't a single problem with a customer that I can't solve. Sure, maybe there's a person who's just never pleased, no matter how hard you try, or they have a problem that can't be solved with glasses. But those are the exceptions. By and large, every person who walks through my doors will walk out thrilled with the service they got, the product they got, and the price they paid. And they always come back. They come back because they know they'll be treated fairly. They'll be treated with respect.

The store opened its doors in 2006. Ten years later, we're still going strong. As I said at the beginning, I've got an amazing staff who really get my vision and are there for me, one hundred per cent. Without them, the store couldn't be what it is, especially these days, now that I've been forced to step back and take more of a back seat. So I can't thank them enough.

It took me a while to find them, though. Finding great staff is a process. You go through a lot of duds before you find people you want to hold on to. I mean, I've had staff who didn't even know how to run basic household appliances. I remember asking this guy if he could boil the kettle for tea, and he was like, "The kettle? How does that work?" I had to show him how to work an electric kettle, if you can believe it. And then one time I had a girl tell me she'd never used a vacuum cleaner. I'm sorry, but what? This customer had come in and accidentally spilled coffee all over the carpet. So I asked her if she could vacuum it up while I did the measurements for his glasses. And she was like, "I've never used one of those—I don't know how it works. Have you got a Dustbuster? I could use that." But I didn't, so she got out the vacuum and I showed her how it worked. Imagine that ("See, this end plugs into the wall. And then, you're going to push this little button right here and—watch. Let me show you. This little thing's going to blow your mind.") I never realized I needed to put those things in a job application: "Must be familiar with basic household appliances." They sure know how to work their smartphones, though. They're hooked up to those things like an IV. You can't separate them. It's enough to drive you mad.

Truthfully, those were small issues, though. I've had bigger ones. I had this one kid on coke. I sort of knew he was on coke, but he told me he was dealing with it. It turned out dealing with it meant sleeping out back by the dumpster and walking into work the next day in the same clothes he'd had on the day before. And then his drug dealer started stopping by...I mean, you can't have that. You just can't have that. It's not good for business. So I had to let him go.

And of course there were the optical students. I've always had students. I always figured after all the time and effort people gave to mentoring me, I could give a little of that back. Plus then the students I train know my system, and I can teach them all the ways that make my store work. But, all too often, you know what happens? Just when I get them trained, get them through their course and so they know all our systems, they decide they can do better elsewhere. So off they go. And all that hard work I put into mentoring and training is wasted, and I have to try again—training someone new, hoping that this student will stick with it, stick with me after all the schooling's done. And on and on it goes.

But some of my staff that I've got now have been there for a good while. Five or seven years, some of them. When you find the good ones, you've got to treat them right and pay them well. Then they tend to stick around. It creates a good vibe in the store, too. Because they actually want to be there. They like coming in to work. It makes things go smoothly.

Finding good staff is just one challenge of running a store. I remember when I first opened, we just kept getting broken into. These guys would break the glass in the front door, come in, rip the cash register out of the cabinet and make off with it. And they'd get, what, maybe fifty bucks? And I'd be out two thousand five hundred. I'd need a new door and a new cash register, a new float, everything. Eventually I got a security system, and that helped some. But it only does so much good. The same kid broke in four times, and the cops did end up catching him, but then he was back on the street awaiting trial! And even if he does get convicted, I'm not getting my money back. Anyway, now I've got special glass on the doors. But that doesn't stop them. Nope, they still break a hole in the glass, trying to get in. And then when they see they can't, they just move on to the next business on the block. I've seen my neighbour the next day cleaning glass from the front of his store, and sure enough, the damn kids broke in there, as well. I'd rather they just came to me and I'd give them the fifty bucks. I'd have saved so much in the end.

I remember I had a break-in at my house in Red Deer, too. I was renting a little house up by the hospital when I was getting the store off the ground, and one night they came and smashed in all the windows in my truck. Didn't take the radio or anything, just grabbed the change from the console. I had to replace all those windows. Man, I sure was keeping the glass guy in business for a while. We got to be on a first-name basis. I should've asked for a bulk discount or something. Anyway, all that to say it didn't stop me. I made it. It wasn't long before the store was doing well enough to handle those bumps in the road.

Building my business was one of the most difficult and challenging things I've ever done. It's super stressful, knowing all these people's livelihoods depend on how well I do what I'm supposed to, how well I look after my responsibilities. But I always knew I would do the work, get things done, and I surrounded myself with people who thought the same. And it shows in our product, in the revenue we generate each year, in the positive experience and feedback of our customers.

In the end, going into business for myself turned out to be a great thing—a really important decision. It freed me. I've only just learned how important that freedom really is, when the troubles of life come calling.

The last little while, I've had to step back. Because I had this whole new battle to face. This fight with my face. But I've got things in place down there. The business is running just fine. Thank God.

I'm determined to take that same attitude of success to this new chapter. That same attitude that went into building my business is what's allowing me to heal my face. At some point, I just decided I was going to figure it out, figure out what was wrong with me. It was up to me. I could do it. And I knew that, one way or another, I was going to find out. I know how to listen to the world. To pay attention. I know how to recognize the truth when I see it. I've been building that skill my whole life.

Chapter 4
Like Something out of a Science Fiction Movie

I remember this one night when I was a kid—the first winter out on the farm, in fact—I saw a comet in the sky. I remember standing out on the back deck in my pyjamas. It was pretty cold. It was still winter, February or March, and it was late in the evening, maybe eleven o'clock. I don't know what I was doing out there, but I remember looking up in the sky and seeing this comet. It was huge. Way bigger than the moon and brighter, too. And it glowed, reddish, like the sun almost. It was absolutely dazzling. Blazing with angelic light. It had a long trail streaming out behind it in the sky, like a pale banner lit from within. And I remember just standing and watching it and feeling so small, so totally in awe. It looked like angel wings spread on the sky, the tail of this comet. It was the most beautiful and terrifying thing I'd ever seen.

And—I distinctly remember this—I went back inside the house, and I got the Bible down from the shelf, and I turned it to the book of Revelations. I stood there in the living room, in my pyjamas, with my feet freezing from being out on the deck, and I read the Bible.

As I was reading it, this warm feeling settled over me, like a cozy blanket or a hug. And I knew in that moment that everything was going to be okay. And I remember just smiling. I closed up that Bible and put it back on the shelf, and I went down the hall to my room and went to sleep. I knew that whatever was happening out there in the sky, whatever magnificence was stirring up in the heavens, I was going to be all right.

The reason I bring this up is I've always had this ability to recognize the truth. When something is true, it just hits me. It hits me hard, right in the gut. And I get what I call "the chills."

The chills is one of those things I didn't realize was special about me. For the longest time, I thought everyone got them like I do. I mean, I know that everyone gets them. But not everyone gets them like I do.

You know that feeling, kind of like goosebumps, when your skin goes cold and your hair stands up on end? Well, I get that all the time. Just waves and waves of it when I recognize things in the world, or make connections between things, or hear someone say something that really resonates. I've always been connected between brain and body like that—really tapped in. As though I'm seeing more than other people.

As a kid, I would get the chills so often I learned how to do it on command. I got to the point where I could just think, "Get the chills, Steve," and I'd get them—get cold and prickly all over like that.

The thing is, though, I never realized that wasn't normal. I just thought everyone could do it. I didn't know it was something unusual. I can still do it on command. I don't do it that often these days, though. It hurts like the dickens, all this stuff I've got in my skin. But sometimes I can't help it; sometimes, when I have those epiphany moments, those moments of revelation, then I get the chills without meaning to.

I think it has to do with being spiritually aware. I'm always noticing how much goes on beyond the physical. I've always been so conscious of that other plane of existence, that spiritual realm. I've always wanted to connect with it, learn about it. That's what the I Ching was about. That's what faith taught me, growing up in my parents' church like I did.

But I learned pretty early in life that just being aware doesn't give you all the answers. You still have to be able to make sense of them. And that isn't always easy to do. Because the tools we have to connect to the spiritual world are subtle. They don't always spell things out for us in black and white.

Let me give you an example. I distinctly remember this one time I was living in Nelson and still pretty early in my days of reading the I Ching.

I was planning to house-sit for Mark, the friend who'd introduced me to the I Ching in the first place. Anyway, the day before I went to see him off, I did a reading. And it wasn't a good reading. While I was sitting and thinking, the canary I had jumped out of its cage and flapped around the room before hitting the coffee table and falling to the floor. When I'd convinced myself it was dead, it jumped up and flew back into its cage again. You have to understand that it had never done anything like that before. It really freaked me out. I didn't like it at all. I'd been sitting there, thinking about the upcoming week, thinking about Mark's trip, and then my bird went totally berserk. Meditating on it, I worried it about what it all meant; I worried it meant Mark was going to die.

When I went to see off my friend the next day, I told him about it. "Look, I'm concerned about you after that, okay? I need you to take extra care on the roads and stuff. You need to promise me you'll drive really carefully," I said.

He just shrugged it off, said he'd be fine, that he'd drive carefully but he'd taken the trip to Vancouver a million times and he was sure everything would be okay.

Well, partway through the week, I was driving out to Mark's place to check on it, and I was coming up to where I had to turn from Highway 3 onto Highway 6. And up ahead I saw this guy hitchhiking, with his thumb out. But as I got closer, he dropped his arm. I thought maybe he'd done so because he heard me slowing down for the turn and he thought he could get a ride with me. But then, as I was passing him, he jumped out in front of me. Like, literally jumped right in front of my car.

Lucky for me, no one was coming the other way, and I swerved and managed to avoid him. But I looked back at him, like "What the heck, man?" and I was shocked for a second because he looked just like Mark. I thought it was Mark at first—they looked so identical.

Anyway, I avoided him, and I slowed down and made the turn onto Highway 6 and drove up to my buddy's place. I was only up there for maybe an hour, and then I headed back to town. But when I got back to the intersection with Highway 3, there were emergency vehicles all over the place: police, ambulance, fire, everything.

I stopped my car and I got out, wanting to see what was going on. One of the RCMP officers came over and told me to get back in the car.

I asked him, "Officer, can you tell me—did some guy jump in front of a vehicle here?"

He looked at me as if I was crazy. "Yeah," he said. "How on earth did you know that?"

"'Cause he tried to do the same thing to me, just over an hour ago."

That experience really shook me. I mean, in and of itself, having someone try to kill himself by jumping in front of your car is nasty. It's pretty scary. But then, to top it off, with the I Ching, I'd known something bad was going to happen. Only I hadn't gotten the details right. It wasn't my friend who was in danger. But it was someone who looked just like him. Or perhaps it was even about me, about nearly killing someone who looked just like him. Maybe it was me in danger, and it wasn't about Mark and his safety at all.

So, mistakes happen. And I was still pretty new at the whole I Ching thing. I was still learning. But I was starting to be able to translate the things I was seeing in the world around me into reflections of how the world worked and what was going to happen next.

A big part of being able to learn about the world around you is knowing about yourself. I'm a big believer in learning about yourself. Maybe that's because I always had this sense that I was different from other people, and I wanted to know why. I always wanted to know who I was, and I had this need to understand my place in the world, my place in the cosmos. And I would try to do that in any way I could.

When I was in Calgary, working toward my contact lens diploma, I went to get an astrology reading done. It was really fascinating, that reading. One of the things I've always felt is that I'm a little bit removed from the world—I see things differently than everyone else. I'm more detached from things—it's like I see them at a distance, almost. Well, that astrology reading told me why: I was born under a new moon. And people born under new moons are entering a new spiritual cycle. They come into this world without the ties and the baggage of their previous lives. It's as if they have a clean slate, if you will. So anyway, when I was born, whatever spirit was born into my body was coming in clean and fresh. I didn't carry all the judgements and hang-ups that a whole lot of spirits bring with them when they're born. So I just don't care about some of the things that other folks get so caught up in. My spirit can't be bothered. It hasn't made the kinds of judgements and assumptions required to care.

I think that's partly why discovering the I Ching was so interesting to me. It let me glean more information about life. It gave me a reason to pay attention, to draw connections between things, to see how the little details of today might be important in the bigger scheme of things.

Anytime you dabble in the spirit world, dig into the real meaning of things, it can get big and weighty pretty fast. One of the things the astrologer told me was that I have a lot of zeal. A lot of fervour. Because I have such a hard time believing in things, when I do believe in them, I believe in them with my whole heart, my whole being. I get so passionate about them that I want to shout them from the rooftops. That's dangerous. Not the shouting, I don't mean that. But the believing like that. Because I can be really harsh with other people. Really judgemental. Impatient. Because I don't get why they don't see what's so obvious to me. What's so right. So I've got to watch out for that.

Another thing that's important to understand about digging into the spiritual realm is that it doesn't always make sense to us. It's really subtle. It's vast and different, and only overlaps with our world in a small way; our physical world is just one manifestation of something much grander. So, as we try to dig in and connect with and interpret that other realm, we get things wrong, like I did with the I Ching that time.

It's tough. But you've got to accept it. Because it's still worth making the effort to see clearly. Then, when life gets tough, and things don't go the way you want them to—or when they just go bad—there's something more to reach for. It's important to remember that there's something more. That we aren't just put on this earth to live and then die. We're here on a journey. Our souls are on a journey, and this little life here on planet Earth is just one teeny, tiny part of that journey. Our physical world is just one tiny manifestation of a vast and unknowable spirit world.

Music is one of the ways the spirit world seems to step right into this one. It's one of those mind-body-soul joiners. When a good song comes on, and your body just starts moving, and you feel the beat pulsing inside of you, and you just can't help but sing—man, that is the best feeling in the world. That's spirit talking. Every time I feel that I wish I played music more. Better. I mean, I took piano lessons when I was a kid, like everyone else, but I didn't get it then. I just thought it was a waste of my time. I wanted to be out riding my bike not sitting down at that stupid keyboard. Silly. If only I'd known.

I first discovered the power of music in high school. I'd tool around in my truck, radio blasting, driving right through the moment, lifted high on those songs. I listened mostly to rock and roll then, AC/DC, Top 40 stuff. Not exactly Beethoven, but it didn't matter; it still moved me. I'm into percussion piano these days; I picked it up from Sir Elton John.

When I lived in Calgary, I did some karaoke singing. Got those tapes with the vocals removed and would sing along to that. Sometimes I would go out to clubs. And before I moved out to Regina I got the chance to write and record a song with some buddies of mine—man, that was amazing. It was never a big hit or anything, but just sitting in a studio, hearing the guitar and the bass and the vocals all coming together to make something magical—there is nothing else like it. I was going through a tough time when that happened; I was dealing with a bad back and felt as if my life was falling apart a little bit, but that song came out of it. I got the opportunity to make some real music. Music can heal, I tell you what. It's like a prayer that's inside of you.

Prayer is another way we brush the spirit world. I don't mean that kind of prayer we all do as kids, the bargaining kind, the selfish kind: "God, I swear I'll pray to you every day if you give me a new bike," or the threatening kind, "God, if you don't make Gordie stop picking on me at recess, I'll never believe in you again!" No, I mean the real kind of prayer—the kind where you open yourself up to God. Where you listen to him and stay open to his will.

I spent a good many years not praying. I forgot about it there for a while. Not forgot, really—I was still turning toward the spiritual in other way—but praying to the God I grew up with just didn't seem important. As my face got worse, though, I turned in prayer toward God a lot. It's funny how in trying times that's all we have left to turn to.

Things with my face were going nowhere. I was getting down about it. Like, really down. It was draining me dry. I had no energy for anything. I just felt exhausted all the time. I could barely get out of bed in the mornings. I slept a lot, but it never felt like it got any better, like I was any less tired. My brain felt slow and fuzzy, as though I was operating in a fog.

As though everything was filtered through a rainy window, making an impression of the world that was blurry and distorted and sluggish. I felt as though I was dragging my way through life every single day. It was as if nothing mattered, nothing was worth doing, because it took such huge effort, colossal effort, to do anything at all.

And all the time I was struggling so hard, I was trying to make sense of life, trying to find my role on the planet. It's pretty hard to feel motivated to find your purpose in life when you're just trying to find a reason to get out of bed. Not exactly inspiring. Not the kind of mindset you want to have.

But I knew that that was part of the problem; I had no sense of purpose. I didn't see why it mattered if I got up and faced the day. Yeah, I wanted to look after the store. Yeah, I wanted to be there for my employees and family and friends who needed me. But I'd made pretty good systems. They didn't really need me all that often.

That went on for months and months. All through the first half of 2015, I'd say. Maybe it even started before that, back in 2014. I don't know. Much of that time blurs together now. But I remember one particular day very clearly. On that day, I was given a whole new perspective.

I remember I went down to the gazebo in my backyard to meditate. I was doing that pretty often; I'd taken to calling it my Godzebo, because it's where I always went to pray. To spend time with my Lord, to meditate on the meaning of my life, my purpose. To say my favourite prayer, Psalm 23: "The Lord is my Shepherd, I shall not want..."

I remember on that particular day, it was raining. I'd been sitting there a while, thinking and meditating, and feeling so completely down—and it got so the rain felt like tears from heaven. Like God was sorrowing in my lack of willingness to do his will.

I was so frustrated. I wanted, more than anything, to find my purpose. To be open enough, to listen well enough, to hear, to truly *know* God's will for me. But I felt so broken, too, because I knew what I looked like. I knew what sort of mess my face had become. I was at the end of my rope. I didn't know how I could do anything good for the Lord looking like a strung-out junkie who no one could ever take seriously.

I'd been out there for hours, and I just felt lost and alone, as if I was cut off from anything good around me. I remember I took my shirt off, and I walked out in the rain and slumped to my knees in despair. Tears streaming down my face, I raised my arms to the heavens and I cried out, "How can I do it, God? How can I do your work in the world when I look like this?" I felt so desperate and isolated and broken. I couldn't imagine an answer, never mind THE answer. I wanted it so fiercely; there I was on my knees in the rain, begging for it.

Instead of an answer, what I felt was this solid certainty that, once and for all, I was going to get to the bottom of this skin condition. Never mind what all the doctors had said over the years—all the diagnoses of stress-related zits, or hormonal acne—those words had gotten me nowhere. This time, I decided, I was going to figure it out on my own. I was going to solve the problem.

It felt like a spark, like a flickering of life in my chest.

With a new drive and real determination, I dragged myself up and went inside. I went straight to my computer, opened up Google, and started to search. I was going to find out this time. I was going to find the answers. I needed to know. I was ready. Really ready.

This time, please God, let the answers come. I've got to fix this. I'm tired of the roller coaster. I'm at the end of my rope. This time I need to know. Please, let me know.

I sat there, staring at that little search box, and again I felt at a loss. How was I going to figure this thing out when I didn't even know where to start? I had no name to go on, no information. So I typed in "Bee-Stinging Acne." That's the nearest I could get to describing this beast. That's what it looked like—acne. That's what it felt like—the sharp, aching itch of a bee sting. Only worse, but Google breaks under too many words. Simple, close, near enough. Bam. Hit Enter. Search.

Go Google. Do your thing.

A whole bunch of results came up. At least that was something. It was not a nonsense search, at the very least. It gave me something to work from.

I clicked on a couple of the links. Not helpful. They didn't tell me anything new, give me any answers, point me in any direction that seemed promising. I'd click, full of hope. Read, and crash with disappointment. Click, hope, crash. Again.

Then I hit on a blog by some guy in the States. He was describing exactly—exactly—what I'd been feeling. The weeping, oozing sores. The lesions. The bits coming out of them, like fibres or tiny, hard crystals, shards of glass. How his skin looked like he had the worst case of acne you've seen in your life. How it ached worse than he could possibly imagine.

This is it, I thought. This is what I've got. I kept reading, wanting to know—what is it? What has he got?

I came to the end. Crash–disappointment. He didn't know. He'd posted it, hoping to find out. He was asking for input.

Might as well read the comments, I figured. Might as well. I haven't found anything else remotely promising.

Lyme disease—nope, not that. Chronic fatigue disorder. Not that, either. Hypersensitiva magnesia. Could be. Keep reading. Morgellons. Never heard of it.

But something about this comment catches my eye. He's insistent, this guy. But not in a rude way. In a way that says he knows what he means. He's sure. He's lived it.

Morgellons, huh? What is that, anyway?

He'd included a link.

I clicked on it and landed on Morgellons.org. I came face to face with all these pictures, pictures of so many people's skin looking just like mine.

This was it. I felt a trickle of certainty down in my gut.

But what was it?

Words jumped off the page. Lesions. Nanotechnology. Fibres. Brain fog. Spiritual journey.

And suddenly I had the chills. I had the chills so hard, my whole body was in a cold sweat. With it came a burst of pain. Man, they hurt! Those lesions hurt something awful when I get the chills.

But I knew, with one hundred per cent certainty that this was it. *This was it. This was it.* I had a name for this thing that was overtaking me: Morgellons. This was what I had.

I poked around some more. I was inspired. I had a starting point. Nothing, nothing was going to stop me now.

I clicked on other sites, other links, and saw all those photos of people's lesions, and the fibres and crystals they pulled out of their skin. If I'd thought my own life was disgusting, it was nothing compared to the state some of these folks were in—massive lesions taking up half their arms. Lesions all down their legs. Man, it was disgusting! But it was familiar, too. I had skin that looked just like that.

I kept pouring over the pages: Morgellonscure.com, Morgellons.ca, reading other survivors' accounts in blogs and posts. I kept looking for some cure, some treatment, something I could do.

I didn't know then what I know now—that this all lands in the realm of conspiracy theory and no one takes it seriously. Back then, I still thought all I needed to do was find a name, and I'd find a cure. That looking online I would find what to do to fix myself, or at the very least, be able to walk into a doctor's office and know what to say to get the help I needed. That there would be a medication I could take, or something I could do to fix my face.

I was so wrong.

According to the websites, no one was taken seriously, even though all these people were clearly struggling with something real. The descriptions and testimonials talked about these aching lesions that grew and grew beneath the skin, burning as if they had shards of glass in them trying to get out. This brain fog that didn't let them focus on anything, leaving them feeling apathetic and down and lost. These people felt quite sure that they were dealing with something unexplained and very, very serious. But what anyone could do about it was hard to say.

I didn't know then that I was just beginning my research, that I'd get to know way more about this diabolical disease than anyone else on the planet. But I did learn a few things that day. And they changed my life.

Chapter 5
So You've Got Morgellons

I can't even describe to you the relief I felt at finally having a label for this thing. At long last, I'd found something. I'd found other people who had common experiences.

That, in and of itself, was the most amazing thing. It was such a gift. Knowing that I was not alone in my struggle gave me strength. And hope. It made me feel like the end of my suffering was near.

And several of the sites had sections devoted to a cure. While there wasn't any magic bullet, or a magic wand to wave that could bring relief, there were recommendations. Things you could do. Actions you could take to relieve the pain.

Finally, *finally*, something I could *do*. Right away I decided I'd try a couple of the recommendations. I mean, I was looking for relief and I would have taken anything—anything—that was thrown at me. But it was also kind of like a test. I wanted to confirm to myself what I already knew. If the recommendations worked, I'd know for sure that Morgellons was what I had.

The very first thing I tried was a super simple, super safe recommendation. I started wearing a magnetic bracelet around my wrist. Several of the sites insisted that wearing a magnetic bracelet would improve your state of mind immensely. It would bring back a renewed sense of energy.

It would lift that brain fog. I figured that was a good place to start. It was a simple enough thing, wearing a magnetic bracelet, and all the sites said it wouldn't do me any harm, as long as I wasn't wearing a pacemaker. And what better place to start than clearing my mind?

I hadn't realized, but magnetic bracelets are pretty commonly available. So I went out to the store, and I bought myself one. The sites said to wear it all the time, even when you were sleeping. Well, except in the shower—you could take it off in the shower. So I just snapped that thing on my wrist and forgot about it. I wore it all day. I even wore it when I went to bed.

Sleep was tough for me then. I knew I really, really needed to sleep, and that made it hard. I'd been so stressed out for so long, battling this thing—resenting feeling tired, hurrying toward dreamland—and that kept my mind from calming down enough to sleep. Plus, these lesions hurt. Those little bits of glass or whatever they are trying to come out from beneath the skin hurt at the best of times, but if there's the least bit of added pressure on them, they sting and ache like crazy.

Have you ever tried sleeping where none of your body will experience any extra pressure? Let me tell you, it's impossible. No matter how you prop yourself up, some of the skin on your head will come into contact with a pillow, or the edge of a chair, or whatever. So sleep was hard. Bedtime was painful. Even when I took pain killers, I couldn't sleep that well. It was an ongoing battle.

That first night I wore the bracelet, I was able to sleep okay. A minor miracle. And the next day I felt a little better; my head didn't seem as foggy as before. I felt such relief over that. The place I was at, any small improvement was worth celebrating. So I kept that bracelet on all day again, and the next night I slept for real. For the first time in I don't know how long.

The next day when I woke up, I had all this energy! I felt like a ten-year-old boy again. I felt so alive. I was just raring to go. I couldn't wait to tackle my day. I bounced out of bed, ready to race outside and run around the block ten times just to contain all my energy. And I could think! I could feel my mind turning over with all the quick dancing tricks I hadn't even realized were missing. Everything was wonderfully sharp.

It was as if my brain had just gotten a new pair of glasses. The brain fog was gone. Gone!

Do you know what a gift that is? To go from exhausted and dragging your feet and everything looking grey to feeling as if you can take on the world? As if anything is possible? It's like Christmas Eve. It's better than Christmas Eve. It's just the most incredible, incredible revelation. I couldn't believe it. I felt saved. No, delivered. I felt delivered from a nightmare.

Well, I went right out and I bought another bracelet. I wanted one on each wrist. If one could make that much of a difference, I figured two would be even better. Man, was I excited.

Even better, my little experiment with the bracelets had pretty much convinced me that I was right. Whatever this Morgellons thing was, that's what I had. So I went back online to try and learn more about what exactly Morgellons was.

Morgellons is not really a disease in the traditional sense. It's not like a virus or an infection or something like that. What it really is—and this seems impossible—is bits of nanotechnology. You know how I keep talking about these things under my skin that feel like glass wanting to push out? These little fibres I find coming out of my skin? Well, they aren't bits of me, after all. They're mechanical. They're tiny tech threads. Bits of miniscule computers in my body.

Do you know what it's like, reading that? Feeling all those little shards digging their sharp little claws into your skin, slicing through your face, pushing out from behind your forehead, and knowing that they're tiny bits of tech? Implants in your skin? Only you never put them there?

I got the creepy-crawlies all over. The heebie-jeebies. I wanted to just burrow inside myself and wrench all those little uninvited monsters right out of my skin.

My second reaction was, *no way. Calm down, Steven--that can't be right. There's no way that's possible.*

But then I started thinking about it. According to the websites, the bracelets work because they draw the mechanical bits away from your brain. Magnets draw metal, I know that. We used to play with magnets on the foundry floor in Delburne. So it totally makes sense that putting magnets on my wrists would help draw these fibres away from my brain.

Doesn't it? And the fibres being away from my brain would help clear my head. And I started thinking about the effect magnets have on computers, or even things like bank cards, how a good magnet can ruin your card.

I got the chills at that, man. Of course my brain can think more clearly now! Suddenly it can think freely again because it doesn't have all this other junk interfering with it all the time! The magnets are disrupting the technology, and it's breaking down!

Another wave washed over me as I realized the horrific truth: The worst of my lesions are on my face, up by my head. No wonder I've had all this brain fog. No wonder I've been so down, swimming in a cloud, barely able to function. It's so obvious now I see it. Duh. My brain's been clouded by all this tech that's worked its way into my body. That's interfering with my brain.

As soon as I learned that—as soon as I really accepted it—I knew I had to get it out. Get the tech out, and I'd be healed. Simple. Obvious solution. But how was I going to do that?

Lucky for me, the websites had a solution for that, too: a borax wash. Given the massive success I'd had with the magnetic bracelets, I was ready to give it a try. I went out and got some borax—people think it's bad for you, or that it's poisonous, but it isn't, as long as you don't drink it. It's just a salt. People use it in their laundry. And this was just taking things a little further. Instead of washing my clothes in it, I was washing myself.

Can I tell you, it was one of the most eye-opening and surreal experiences I've ever had? I followed the instructions I found on the Morgellonscure website, and it left me in no doubt, absolutely no doubt, that my skin is infested with these things. If you're a Morgellons sufferer, too, this is a really, really important step to take, and I urge you to try it. It'll jump-start your recovery like nothing else.

Here's what I did, following the instructions as I found them on Morgellonscure.com. I took a big cup—a giant plastic one, the type you'd use for a Slurpee when you were a kid. I took that cup and I filled it about halfway with borax. Then I filled the rest with hot water, and I stirred it all up, dissolving a bunch of the borax. Then I got myself all undressed, and I stood in the shower, and I splashed that borax water all over my skin. Whenever the water level in the cup would get a bit low,

I'd add some more hot water and I'd mix it up some more, and I'd keep splashing it all over my body.

Once I was good and wet, and my skin had had a chance to soak, I rubbed my skin down. Lightly, using a slight bit of finger pressure, I pressed over my skin. And as I pressed, this fine grit, like sand, came out from under my fingers.

I was freaking right out at that. Like, losing my mind creeped. But I was determined. I was going to rid my body of these little tech invaders. I was going to get them out of me right then and there. So I pressed and I pressed, lightly of course, brushing my fingers all over my skin, all over every inch of me. And all the while out came this fine, gritty, sand-like stuff. From all over. All over my skin. It was disgusting. Horrifying. I've never had such a visceral reaction to anything in my life. I nearly vomited in the tub.

Imagine brushing this alien grit out of your skin, grit from *nowhere*. And I could see it collecting in the bottom of the tub. It wasn't as if it came off and then just disappeared. It piled up until I couldn't handle it anymore, at which point I rinsed my whole self down, and the bottom of the tub, as well. I had to get rid of it, had to eliminate whatever these things were that had found their way into my being.

But I didn't think I was done. Every time I'd pressed my skin, more grit would come out. So I refilled the cup with borax, and I did it all over again. Four separate cups full of borax I used. Four cups. Four times, I stirred up the borax in the cup, splashing the hot water and borax all over myself, stirring and splashing until the cup was empty. Four times, I pressed my fingers along my skin, working out whatever little bits of grit were stuck in there. Four times, I rinsed down the tub to rid it of the sand. Each time the grit got a little less. By the fourth time, I could hardly feel any more grit at all.

By the time I finished that fourth round and showered down, I was exhausted. But as I toweled off, I touched my skin, and my jaw just about hit the floor. My skin was so, so soft. Like new-born-baby-bottom soft. Just silky and fresh and clean and new. I felt like a million bucks.

Finally, *finally*, I knew what was wrong with me. I felt hopeful, exhilarated, as if now I could cope. I knew what I was facing, and I had some tools to deal with it. I had the magnetic bracelet, and now the borax wash.

I fully planned to keep using those. But I wondered if there was anything else I could do.

So I poked around some more and discovered a third thing: drinking baking soda. That's another gem from Morgellonscure. What you do is you dump a teaspoon or two into a tall glass of water, and you stir it up, and you drink it. It's another one of those things that the Morgellons fibres don't like. It doesn't impact your body in any way. It's not going to hurt you. But it makes your body an environment that Morgellons doesn't want to live in.

I was early into my research, and I already had quite a routine. I'd drink a glass of baking soda every day. Sometimes twice a day—in the morning and at night. I'd wear those magnetic bracelets all the time, too, one on each wrist. And I'd repeat that borax wash about once a week. Every time I tried it, I'd get a bunch of gritty fibres coming out of my skin, but never as many as that first time. I'd usually only need one or two cups of borax to get the sandy stuff out.

For the first time in a long time, I could cope. I just knew I was on the path to getting better. Finally, after all this time, I'd managed to set myself on a path toward healing.

Chapter 6
The Whole World is Infected

After that first borax wash, I combed the Internet for anything and every-thing I could find about Morgellons. I learned a lot. Let me tell you, none of it is very nice. As I put more and more pieces together, as I discov-ered what I was really dealing with, I started getting an uneasy, gnawing feeling in my stomach. As if my nerves were bubbling up through my guts. Every day I lived with that—this repulsion and horror at what I was learning. It really was horrific.

One of the biggest questions I had early on was whether I was con-tagious or not. I really needed to know: Was I going to infect anyone else? Because let me tell you, I was determined not to pass this terrifying and horrific experience on to the people I knew. There was no way in a million years that I was going to drag the people I care about into this world of pain. I wouldn't do that to my worst enemy, never mind the people I most love and respect.

So I made that my starting point: Am I contagious? Does Morgellons spread?

Here's what I found.

Morgellons has already infected the entire planet. Every single person on earth already has Morgellons.

I know you're thinking, *Yeah, right. I'd know if I had anything like that disease you're talking about. My face is fine. My skin is fine. I don't have little fibres inside me trying to get out.*

But here's the hard truth: That doesn't mean a thing. The things I've been describing—brain fog, lesions—those are only symptoms. And all those symptoms are saying is that my body's fighting this infestation. That's all. I mean, yes it means that I have Morgellons. We're agreed on that. But your lack of symptoms doesn't mean you don't have Morgellons; it just means you're not fighting it.

I know it's an ugly fact. It sounds horrific and your first response is to reject it. But just imagine for a second that it's true. Let yourself think about it long enough to let the horror of it sink in: Every single person on earth is infected. Every single one of us.

That's appalling. Horrific. I can't imagine anything worse.

It made me angry. Really upset. But it also made me focused. I was determined to figure out how in the world this had ever happened.

I pushed on. I kept researching. That was the only way I was going to get to the bottom of things. And everything I learned—it just kept getting worse and worse and worse.

You have to understand. Morgellons isn't a disease in the usual sense. It's not a virus, or a bacterial infection, or any of the other conventional things medicine would tell you it could be. It's a totally foreign substance. The fibres that people pull out of their skin are not comparable to any other substance on the planet. *Any other substance!* They have a structure that's totally outside the realm of life as we know it.

I learned this from watching a woman named Sofia Smallstorm on YouTube. She has studied Morgellons fibres very closely, examining them under a microscope and stuff, and what she discovered is totally mind-blowing. She explained how Morgellons fibres don't have a structure like anything else in the scientific tree of life. The way the fibres are built—they aren't eukaryote structures *or* prokaryote structures, the two basic ways cells can be organized. They aren't either. They are something completely and totally new.

So, how does something that shouldn't even exist on earth come to infect every human being on the planet? Well, it's a bit of a long explanation.

See, Morgellons comes from what you might know as chemtrails. You know those twin white clouds that come out behind airplanes? Contrails? Well, have you ever noticed how they're different than they were when we were kids? How they linger in the sky and spread and spread and spread? That's because they aren't just moisture anymore—they're chemicals, too.

Here's what happens. Airplanes—big jets, commercial airliners that fly all over the world—spew chemicals while they fly. That's part of what's in the white clouds behind airplanes; it's what makes them behave differently than they used to. And those chemicals that get dispersed behind the jets, they spread all over the earth, everywhere planes fly. Which is pretty much everywhere, except maybe Antarctica. I don't know if Antarctica is infected with Morgellons. I don't know if anyone has gone to check.

Well, planes spreading chemicals all over the world is bad enough. It's terrible, really, that our governments would allow that. Beyond terrible. Catastrophic! How can that happen? But is has happened. It's still happening. It's a catastrophe of global proportions.

But that's not even the worst of it. What's worse is all those chemicals are made up of what's called "smart dust." They're teeny, tiny little pieces of technology, the tiniest computers you can imagine. Maybe a couple of molecules big. Which in and of itself sounds like no big deal, right? Here's where it gets scary: They accumulate. They work together. They find each other, and the molecules connect. They execute whatever instructions they've got on board, and they get bigger. And then they find another molecule or two, or maybe another cluster that's gotten together, and they all join up. And pretty soon you're dealing with a computer that's not so tiny. Maybe now it's big enough to actually see. So you see what happens? All over the world there are these little computers gathering together, getting a little bit bigger and a little bit bigger and a little bit bigger—until they're big enough to do real damage.

And these little bits of accumulated smart dust, they can live in just about any environment. They can live inside my body. And that's what's happening to me. These little bits of nanotechnology are assembling inside me, and they're building up these little fibres, and that's what my body is trying to reject. My body is pushing them out. Those are the little fibres that are coming out of my skin. Their little computers. Nanotechnology. Disgusting, eh?

When I learned about that, it totally lined up with that experience in the tub with the borax wash. All those little sandy, gritty bits—now I knew what they were. They were bits of nanotechnology, nearly invisible little fibres, the size of a grain of sand, that hadn't assembled into their bigger forms yet. Do you know how hideous it is to know that? To have experienced that coming out of your body?

And that nanotechnology is everywhere! It's in every single one of us! Those tiny computers are assembling inside all of us, only most people don't know it. Did you know you have little bits of nanotechnology, little tiny computers, moving around inside your body? Isn't it horrifying? Doesn't it make you angry?

It makes me angry. So angry. I don't want this. I didn't ask for this. I feel totally betrayed—as if everything I've ever enjoyed about the world has turned sour. I keep thinking about every time I've been out in nature, wandering and savouring the beauty of the world. Every time I caught a fish out of the river and ate it, sure I was eating something fresh and unspoiled. And it wasn't true! I was eating something infested with smart dust, ingesting all these little bits of technology ready to build up inside me.

I boiled in anger over it. I couldn't understand how anyone could let this happen. I really just didn't get it. Someone, probably in government somewhere, had decided that they didn't mind destroying the planet if there was something in it for them.

I've run across that kind of selfishness before, back when I was working in optical in Saskatchewan. For a while I ran a store that was part of a national chain, and the people running that chain—man, they were the worst kind of petty tyrants you can imagine. The company had this commission policy that was pretty straightforward. Every employee got an hourly wage, but there were commission elements, too. Sell a particular kind of frame, you'd get an extra five bucks on your check. Sell anti-reflective coating on the lenses, an extra dollar fifty. That kind of thing. We had to keep a file with all the records in it and such, but come pay cheque we'd get our regular salary plus any of these bonuses we'd earned.

Well, it didn't take me long to realize that the bonuses coming through weren't the same as the bonuses my employees were expecting. Sometimes they'd be right. But as often as not they'd be fifty, eighty, one hundred dollars short. We'd be expecting one hundred and fifty dollars, and would get one hundred and twenty. Expecting one hundred, and get sixty or seventy-five. They weren't even following their own system!

I figured it was just an oversight, so I pointed it out, and my boss said he'd look into it. That was the end of that, I thought. It'd clear up. Only it didn't. My employees were still getting short-changed on their cheques. So I kept asking and asking about it, but all I ever got from my boss was him saying he'd see what he could do.

After a while, I got tired of that game. I started asking the other store managers if that was happening to them. We'd have retreats once a year or so—down in the Caribbean or out east by Niagara Falls, or whatever—and I got to know some of the other managers. So I asked them if there was any discrepancy between what their employees had earned for bonuses and what they were actually getting. Well, no one knew for sure, but a bunch of them said they'd go back and look when they returned to work.

One woman in Ontario was a real ally. After she got home, she'd gone through all the backlog of paperwork and found out I was right. Man, was she pissed! She raised a real stink over it, too, pushing hard for some kind of leveling, trying to get management to pay what they'd agree to. The head honchos, they just kept saying they'd deal with it, they'd deal with it. Only they never did. But she and I kept pushing. It was between one thousand five hundred and two thousand dollars owed to some of us by that time, and we wanted our money.

She was in a big Ontario store, not some start-up out west, so I guess that's why they listened to her. Or maybe we just pushed long enough and hard enough. Anyway, whatever the reason, the upper management folks finally came to their senses and decided they'd had enough of our bitching and that they'd better deal with it. They told us they were doing a system-wide audit to see how much back pay everyone was missing. If they found out anything was missing from that, they'd cut us all cheques.

Surprise, surprise, that audit took forever—another six or eight months. And they found—obviously—that we were right; employees had been short-changed on pay. So they did actually send us some money, but it was only for the current fiscal year—not everything before that, back when we'd first noticed and started making a stink. And they only ended up giving back pay to anyone who was still employed with the company. Which wasn't many people anymore, I can tell you. Employees are smart. They learn pretty quickly when they're not valued, and they go find another job.

So, in the end, the people at the top of that organization weaseled out of having to pay a bunch of money to a bunch of folks, stiffing their hardworking employees money they promised to pay...for what? So some CEO could get an extra-fat cheque? That eighy dollars or one hundred dollars a pay cheque would've meant a lot to someone working for ten or twelve bucks an hour. But instead it went to pad the pockets of some guy who was already wealthy. What a joke.

There were other problems with that optical chain, too. The vendor that the company used for their anti-reflective coating on the lenses was just the worst. They were terrible. That stuff was meant to be guaranteed for two years, but it would always come off. And I liked to recommend it—it's good stuff, that coating. Keeps your lenses reflection-free, makes it way easier to see in any kind of light, and it hardly cost anything extra. Why wouldn't you recommend a product like that? It's a win-win for everyone. Or, it would've been a win-win almost anywhere else.

But the trouble was this company the optical chain used to do the coating was the cheapest one around. So the quality of that coating was terrible. And I mean *terrible*. I'd have the same person come back into my store again and again and again to get their lenses replaced. It got so I'd just want to hide under the desk when some of my customers came in.

Now, I'd complained to management about it. I'd pointed it out. And the company said they'd fix it. So I told my customers that; I trusted the word of the people above me. But big surprise, nothing changed! Same crappy stuff as before, and this after I'd told my customers, promised them to try one more time, that management swore they'd fixed it, and so on. Man, it sucked.

I tried to raise a stink about it, get them to change their mind. I even brought a whole box of the faulty lenses on one of those manager trips because I wanted everyone to see how bad it was. And one or two other managers cared, but mostly people just laughed. The company insisted that even with all the cost to replace the faulty lenses, it was still cheaper and they weren't going to change. They called me "the picky son of a bitch". All because I was trying to get a fair deal for my customers, so they wouldn't have to come in and get new lenses put in their frames every year. Those lenses might be replaced free of charge, from the anti-reflective coating company, but it was still a hassle, and it still took up my customers' time. How was that fair?

That the lenses were replaced by the coating company is one of the things that everyone kept pointing out to me when I tried to make a stink about it. The lenses were being replaced, so what did I have to complain about? Well, they were being replaced, in a way. But the costs for those lenses was returned to the company as a whole, and it was distributed out to all the franchises evenly. Every single store in the country got the same rebate for faulty lenses. Every single one! Even though some sold almost none of the coated lenses, they'd still get money from *my store* because I sold so many of those lenses to my customers. And they'd call me the picky son of a bitch while I was lining their pockets. Nice, eh?

I figure I must have done something right, though, because those guys in upper management sure didn't like me much. You know how I know? Every year, there'd be sales competitions across the country, and there were all these different categories—most frames sold, most multiple frame sales, most sales of a particular type of lens, etc. Well, one year, I won five categories. Every category was supposed to come with its own prize—a proper jacket with the company logo on it. Well, that year, everyone else who won more than one category got more than one prize. I didn't. At the national meeting where they awarded the prizes, they called me up, introduced me as "that picky son of a bitch," and gave me one jacket. One. That's how I know.

Anyway, after they finally settled the whole pay cheque issue, I was done. I stayed on for a few more weeks, but I put my ear to the ground, got in touch with old friends and contacts in the College of Opticians of Alberta, and found myself a different job with a different company. A person doesn't need to be treated the way I was being treated there— making other people's lives difficult just because they can, because it puts a few more dollars in their pockets. I had no patience for that.

I wish I could walk away from this whole Morgellons mess that easily. I wish it were as simple as moving somewhere else. Trust me, I'd do it. I'd be out of here so fast. But there's nowhere to go. There's nowhere on earth that's safe. That's pure and unspoiled, where Morgellons can't live. So I'll have to bear it. I'll have to keep fumbling towards a cure.

But I tell you, while I'm doing that, I am for damn sure going to keep digging. I'm going to keep learning about who got me into this mess. And how I can hold them accountable. Now that I know what's going on, I swear to God I won't rest until I can do something about it.

I know that sounds corny. But I am absolutely determined. And I don't break promises to myself. Not when they matter this much. Not when it's about life and death. I know, because I've done it before. I know, because I've gotten myself into pretty stupid messes before, and gotten myself out of them by keeping my word to myself. The only reason I'm alive at all, and facing this at all, is because I keep my promises.

Back when I was working towards my contact lens diploma in Calgary, before I moved to Nelson B.C, I got into a bit of trouble. I had an old friend from high school who was living in CowTown then, and he'd come over to my place to party every now and again. And, well, he had a connection to a little habit that I'm afraid I let myself get drawn into. I'm not proud of it. I was always a believer that you should take care of your body. That each of us ought to be responsible for what we put into it, treat it like the holy vessel it is. But this old friend of mine had a chemical friend called cocaine, and I'd take a hit of it now and again. Like I said, I'm not proud of it. But I'd let him bring his friends over to my place and party, and he'd give me some stuff in return. I never paid for any of it. And it didn't go too badly. Except for one day.

I'd been feeling a little guilty over my little chemical dabblings, so I didn't hang out with my friend much anymore. But one night he insisted on coming over, saying he hadn't seen me in forever. Eventually, I gave in. I told him, fine, he could come over, as long as he left by midnight, because I had to get up the next day to work. I was due to work at noon. Needless to say, that didn't happen. Before I knew it, it was 11:45 a.m. the next day, and there we were. We hadn't slept, and my heart was pounding as thought it was going to burst out of my chest. I felt terrible and nauseous and had such a bad headache that I could hardly see. The idea of sitting through a shift at work was absolutely terrifying. I didn't think I was going to be able to do it.

So I called in sick. Said there was no way I could make it in, that I felt terrible. Well, that didn't go down too well. I was supposed to close the store that night. After some arguing, I said I figured I might be able to make it in for six. So I kicked those guys out of my place, had something to eat and slept for a little bit, maybe from three until five. Then I got up, showered and went to work.

It was the most horrific shift I've ever worked. I was still feeling terrible, shaky and nauseous, and my heart was beating like crazy. I was sure every single one of my customers could hear it. I was sure that all they needed to do was look at my face and see what I was going through.

But I made it. I made it until nine, and I shut down the store, and when I got home I vowed I would never, ever touch the stuff again. And I haven't. All those years, and I've never touched cocaine since. Nor any other chemical drug.

And it's a good thing I can keep promises to myself. Remember that friend I had in Nelson, Mark, for whom I was house-sitting? Well, while he was away, he'd invited me to make myself right at home in his house. And he had a little stash of the green herb in a box up in his cupboard, and he told me I could help myself. So I took the box down and was going through it, and I found this container of white powder; it looked just like coke.

Well, I was surprised; I hadn't known he was into that. And seeing it there, in the box, a little voice in my head popped up in my head and started nudging me. *Go on, Steven. No one will ever know. There's enough stuff here for a line or two. It's a perfect opportunity. There's no one around. You don't have to work tomorrow.*

But I remembered the promise I'd made myself, and I left it there. I fished out what I came for, and I rolled myself a joint, and I sat on his couch and had a smoke, relaxed, listened to some music, and that was that.

A couple weeks later, when Mark was came back, I confronted him about it. "Hey, Mark, I, uh, saw a little bit of the white stuff there, in your pot locker. I didn't know you were into coke, man."

He gave me this funny look, and he said, "It's not coke, man. It's heroin."

I just went cold all over, hearing that. Heroin? "Good thing I didn't snort any then, huh?" I said, playing it cool, even though I could feel my heartbeat tripping.

"Yeah, man," he said, looking at me, shaking his head. "If you had, you'd be dead."

A close shave like that is enough to scare anyone straight. I mean, I was already running straight—I'd made a decision that honoured my word, and it saved my life. But I never needed that to happen more than once.

And I don't need it now. I know that I'll do everything I can to beat this Morgellons thing, and I know that I'll do everything I can to find out the people responsible, and hold them accountable for the way they've destroyed this beautiful, God-given earth. Knowing what I know now, I couldn't do otherwise.

Chapter 7
No One Listens

Telling people you have Morgellons does not go over well.

I know, in a really intimate sort of way, that people don't want to hear this stuff. I've lost friends over it. I sat down with one of my best friends from childhood—one of the people who knows me the best in the whole world, who has been through all sorts of ups and downs with me, who has seen me at my best and at my worst. I sat down with him and told him about my disease, about Morgellons, and he flat-out refused to believe it. He laughed in my face. Told me I was off my rocker. Didn't believe a word. Not sure how that's possible, because the first thing he did was ask me about my face. He could see it was rotten, as usual. But he didn't want to hear what I had to say.

He argued with me about it for a while, told me all the thousand reasons why it couldn't be true. And when I told him everything that I'd learned about it, he just got up and he left. He left me alone with my truth, in my own pain and agony, simply because he wasn't ready to believe it. Some friend, huh? Throwing away a whole lifetime of friendship because he didn't want to upset his nice little bubble.

I get why. It's a really ugly truth. People don't want to hear it. They don't want to hear that their entire world is affected by this hideous disease. You probably think I'm crazy. Most people do. It's easier.

But here's the thing. Ignoring stuff because you don't want to hear it, or because it gets in the way of your nice little life, or because you're too wrapped up in the day-to-day minutia of getting Johnny to hockey or Susie to piano lessons...that's just wrong. Think about that for a moment. You reject what is true simply because it isn't convenient. Or because you don't like it.

Now, truth is one of those words that's out of fashion. Not only the word, but the concept, too. For my parents, things were either true or not. They had a clear sense of right and wrong. For them, the Bible was their guide on that, and that's because for them, the Bible was the truth.

These days, people talk about truth as though it's malleable. They talk about "my" truth. Or they talk about what they "feel" is true. But the thing about truth is something is either true or it isn't. It isn't true for one person and not true for someone else. Sure, we all have our own different experiences, and those things make us unique. But there are certain things in the world that are just true. The sky is blue. The grass is green. We all know these things. You can't pretend the grass is orange. Well, I guess you could, but you wouldn't be right. It wouldn't be true. It wouldn't even be true for you.

The truth doesn't care what you think of it. Hiding your head in the sand doesn't get you anything. It just makes life harder for you, and for everyone around you, too. And your justification is that you were too busy to care? Too lazy to learn about it? What sort of reasoning is that? Who wants to live in a world where that's normal? That's acceptable? Where you just toss out the information you don't like? Where you ignore it? I don't want to live like that. I reject that. I live in the truth, however uncomfortable it is. And the truth is Morgellons exists. Whether you like it or not.

Anyway, when my friend walked out, I made sure to learn something from that. I realized I had to be way more careful about what I shared with people. Too much information just shut them down. So now I only tell them the general gist of things. I provide the basic foundation: This is a disease of nanotechnology, spewed by chemtrails and airplanes in the sky. It's real, and it affects everyone, and there's really nothing you can do about it but keep living your life. I don't get into some of the crazier details. Because it's just too much for most people.

The more I learn, though, the more I'm determined to share all the things I've come to know. Obviously, I had to share it with friends and family. I had to share it with my employees. I was adamant about that, and I still am. People need to get it.

But how do you get through to people who don't listen? Because that's what happens. People don't listen. They literally just shut down. They switch off. It's as if I've suddenly ceased to exist, and the sounds coming out of my mouth are alien babble.

I used to be so confused by that. But I get it now. If they listen, then they might have to know something they don't want to know. And if they know something they don't want to know, then they might have to take action. And if they have to take action, then their comfortable little lives as they know them will be over. *Over*. And so no one listens. It's easier not to.

Part of the reason nobody believes me about Morgellons is because of the CDC study from about ten years ago. The CDC—the Center for Disease Control in the U.S.—ran this big study back in 2008, because there was such an outcry from Morgellons patients. So many people were suffering from the same symptoms that the U.S. government commissioned a study in California to figure out what was going on.

And you know what they found? Nothing. Actually nothing. They couldn't find any root cause for all these people's horrific experiences. Or at least, not one they were willing to identify. So you know what they decided? That decided that we were all making it up. That we were all one hundred per cent crazy. That's what the official decision came down as.

What they decided is that we must all have a psychiatric disorder called delusional parasitosis. It's a disease where people experience the sensation of bugs crawling under their skin—only the bugs aren't really there. It's all in the sufferers' minds. And the big CDC study in 2008 claimed that if all these people who thought they had "Morgellons" would only stop scratching at these imaginary bugs, then their skin would heal and there wouldn't be a problem. In other words, it was our own fault we looked like this and we should just get our heads on straight and stop bothering everybody else about it. Either that or we needed to be on anti-psychotic medication to make us all okay again.

Isn't that awful? I mean, how does that solve anything? Telling people they're crazy. All that decision did was make everything worse. Now Morgellons sufferers can't talk about what they're actually experiencing, because if they do they'll end up labeled crazy, or stuck in a mental institution. And if any doctors dare to actually listen, and to treat them properly, they're banned from the profession! Yes, it's true. Health practitioners in the United States are losing their licence to practise medicine if they treat people for Morgellons. Unbelievable.

I would have been surprised about the medical community doing something so damaging, if I hadn't heard about tactics like that before. But they've always been like that, sitting on information they don't like, directing us to see certain things so that doctors and pharmaceutical companies can make money off our suffering.

When I was in Regina, a customer of mine came into the store one day and handed me this book.

"You seem like a good guy, Steven," he said. "You've helped me out so much, with my glasses and everything, I thought you might like to have this. That you'd get a lot out of it." And he handed me this book with a bright pink cover.

I took it, of course. I was all like, what the heck? But I took it. I took it, and I read it; it was the least I could do. Glad I did, too. It was fascinating, a real eye-opener. It was called *The Cure for All Diseases*, and it's written by Dr. Hulda Regehr Clark.

Dr. Clark explains that all chronic diseases are caused by parasites in the body. Cancer, diabetes, heart disease, you name it. Parasites get into our bodies through our environments and disrupt our otherwise healthy state. This happens to all of us.

She discovered, though, that each parasite has a unique resonant frequency, and you can zap them dead by sending waves of that frequency through your body. Essentially, you electrocute the parasites.

This may sound like you have to electrocute yourself, but you don't really. You just send a low voltage pulse of particular frequencies through your body, and it kills the parasites (including viruses and bacteria) that are making you sick. Because the voltage is so low, it doesn't affect you at all, really. You can't even feel it. It just kills the parasites. It's incredible!

She figured all this out doing research in her own home. Just paying attention to the world around her and trying different things. And what she realized is that the medical community is holding the world hostage for profit. They don't care what the truth is, they just want to make money. And if that means keeping people sick and in the dark, then so be it. It's not about listening and trying to cure people. It's not about justice or what's right or anything. It's about creating a nice, tidy system that works for the people who made it. And that's the doctors and the drug companies. They keep us all in the dark to pad their own pockets, to make themselves important.

I'd love to say this is something exclusive to the medical community, but it's not. It's not even exclusive to Morgellons sufferers. It's everywhere. People with authority everywhere are abusing their power. They decide what they want to see, and then they make everyone else around them agree with what they see. Even if it isn't true. Even if it isn't right or just.

I've experienced that firsthand, when I was pretty young. Back when I was living in Calgary, after I'd left Interstate Engineering, the vacuum company. I'd been in a six-month lease in Calgary, but I negotiated a way out, and I moved back to the farm to look for work around Red Deer. But then, the roommate I'd been living with stopped paying the rent. He skipped town. So the landlord came after me, and I had to pay outstanding rent and damages. And there was no work in Red Deer anyway, so I moved back down to Calgary. I needed a job.

I was living with a couple of roommates. One of them was a guy I knew from Interstate, and the other guy was his brother. I found work in a pizza place, and that was kind of okay. But then things got weird.

The brother, he came home with a set of tires one day. We asked where he got them, and he was all like "Oh, yeah, they're from this guy's truck, but he got new ones so he gave these to me. I was thinking I'd go down to the mechanics and sell 'em."

Fine, whatever, we didn't think about it much. But a day or two later he came home with a couple hundred dollars. We wanted to know where he got it from, and he said he'd taken two of the tires down to the mechanic's shop just over the way, and that we should take the other two the next day—we could keep the money.

We thought, why not? We could sure use the cash. So we took the tires down to the mechanic shop and tried to sell them. Guess how well that went down? Yeah, major backfire. He wouldn't buy them. He wouldn't even touch them. Worse, he got on the phone as soon as we brought them in, telling us he'd be with us in a minute.

We asked, "What's up? It's no big deal. We just want to sell these tires. You bought two others from our friend the other day."

That's when he dropped the bomb on us. He said, "I think these tires are stolen property."

We split. We ran out of there as fast as we could. But that wasn't the end of it. Oh, no. The mechanic got my licence plate number and called the cops. Next thing you know, my sister called me from the farm, saying the police wanted to talk to me. So I went and talked to the cops, thinking I could just explain it all, how my friend gave us these tires and said if we sold them we could keep the cash.

I might as well have been talking to a couple of posts. They didn't listen to a word I had to say. Instead they charged me with possession of stolen property! Well, I said I'd plead guilty to having the tires—I known they were stolen, of course, but still, I'd had them. But that wasn't enough for them. They wanted to charge me with possession of stolen property over five thousand dollars. Apparently, the friend I was staying with, his friend had stolen not only the tires but a bunch of parts from an auto dealership, and they were going to stick me with the whole lot!

They tried me. I had to go up in front of a judge. And I explained how I didn't know what was happening, and I'd plead guilty to having the tires, but that was all. I was just the driver; I didn't have anything to do with it! It didn't matter what I said, though. They convicted me anyway. Sentenced me to one day in jail and a year's probation. Gave me a criminal record over some stupid tires because they needed to stick someone with the stolen property. It wasn't right, it wasn't just, but that's what happened.

You'd think an organization like the cops would care about truth and justice. But no. I've had more success pushing back at companies than I did with those guys.

I remember when I was working down in Calgary studying for my contact lens diploma, I found out after a few months that my colleagues with fewer qualifications than I had were getting paid more than I was. If I had to guess, I'd say it had to do with my transferring from the Red Deer store—people up there were just getting paid less, and when I came down to Calgary, they kept me on the same salary and I didn't think anything of it. Until I found out that my less-qualified coworkers were out-earning me. That didn't sit so well.

I went and asked my boss for a raise. Just enough of a raise to be at the same level as everyone else. I didn't think it was fair that I was earning less, especially with more qualifications. My boss said it wasn't up to him. It was up to his boss, the bigwig at the corporate offices downtown.

So I went to see the corporate manager downtown in one of those big fancy offices. I'd made an appointment and everything, and he knew what we were going to talk about. But he kept me waiting a long time. Close to two hours, I'd say. I sat there, waiting, my hands all clammy, going over the notes I'd made for myself in my head, wanting to present my case well.

When he finally got around to seeing me, you know what the first thing he said was? "Wow, you look like someone shot you right between the eyes!" I had a big zit forming there—looking back, I realize it was more of a lesion like I get now than a zit like I got in high school—and it was all red and blotchy. It was Stampede week—the crazy cowboy festival that engulfs downtown Calgary for ten days in July—so, no wonder some stupid cowboy joke was the first thing he thought to say. But what a comment. That definitely took the wind out of my sails, I can tell you.

I went in, anyway, and I sat down and asked for my raise. I had to argue from one end of the point to the other and back. And keep in mind I wasn't asking for more than anyone else. I was just asking to get paid the same as my colleagues, even though I should probably have been making more. After sitting and talking with him for an hour, I wrangled my extra few bucks an hour out of him. I got put on a level with the rest of my colleagues. I was more qualified than they were, but at least I wasn't earning less anymore. And at least he listened! Not like those cops.

All in all, that store treated me pretty well, actually. That stint in Calgary was pretty good. I had an apartment right across the street from Chinook Centre so I was able to walk to work and walk home for lunches, even. It was great.

I learned a lot from Glen, my store manager there. I still find myself doing things that I learned while I was working for him. He was a good mentor. Old school, but good. I had a handful of coworkers who were taking the contact lens course with me, and we learned a lot from each other, and a lot from Glen. I try to model a lot of his mentorship ideas for my own optical students who have come through my store, because he always treated us with respect.

He did a few crazy things, too. Once, I think it was on Christmas Eve, he was closing the store, and later, on Christmas Day, I heard sirens coming to the mall. Looking out, I saw it was fire engines. I didn't think much of it, just thought "Oh, yeah, things got a little crazy in there on Christmas." But then I went in on Boxing Day, and it was our store that had needed the fire trucks; Glen had left the tint machine on, and it overheated and started a chemical fire.

Everything was a mess. The carpets were soaking wet, anything on the counters was sopping. And the whole place was covered in soot. Even the stuff in the drawers had soot on it. But we still had to work. I'll never forget that shift, trying to help customers with glasses, having to clean the soot off every single pair, sloshing around on that wet carpet all day. That was something else. To this day, I never leave the shop without checking: Is the tint machine off?

Those years in Calgary were an interesting time. I had a girlfriend when I was there. She was crazy. She kept trying to buy my love. Whatever she thought she could buy for me, she'd buy it. It's almost as if she needed to have me in her debt.

She was really insecure, too. She had these health problems and kept having to get surgery, so she had all these scars all over her torso. She was convinced they made her ugly; she was unbearably ugly in her own eyes. The scars didn't matter to me. I just liked her. I thought she was beautiful. I mean, I didn't even see them after a while—I just saw her. But, anyway, she was really insecure and felt she wasn't good enough, so she'd do crazy stuff to make up for it. I remember this one time we were going out for dinner, and she came to pick me up wearing this nice black coat. It wasn't until we got to dinner that I realized she was wearing *only* the coat. She didn't have anything on underneath. And I mean, anything.

She was totally naked underneath it. Who does that? Funny how stuff like that sticks with you.

I liked her quite a lot. I told her all the time how much I loved her. But I guess she didn't believe me. Kept buying me stuff, as if she had to secure my love. This one time, I was planning a vacation with some friends but didn't end up having enough money to go, so I was going to pull out. She gave me the money, though. She called it a loan, said I could pay her back. But I knew she'd never really expect me to pay it back. She was just trying to tie me up again.

It got so I couldn't handle it. I broke up with her after a while, because I didn't feel as if she really cared about me, or what I thought. She didn't value anything I said; she just kept trying to buy me with stuff. So I broke it off.

That did not go down well. She tried everything she could to get back with me. One time, I was sitting at home before I went to work and the buzzer went. I figured it was her, because she'd tried to call me not long before. I didn't answer it. I had no interest in seeing her.

Not long after that, I heard a knock at my door. I ignored that, too, and then, would you believe, I heard keys jingling and turning in the lock! She'd gone to get the super to let her in. I was really mad at that. As soon as he saw I was in there, he started apologizing, saying he hadn't realized I was there and that the young lady had forgotten her keys and he was just letting her in to get them.

While he was talking, she was trying to sneak in behind him to get into the apartment. Well, I was having none of that. I came right over to the door and made sure she didn't get in. And then I told the super in no uncertain terms that she didn't have keys and never would. Seeing as she couldn't get in and couldn't talk to me, she left, and when she was gone I went down to the superintendent and told him he was not, under any circumstances, to let anyone into my apartment, ever. He apologized and said he recognized her, thought she was genuine. So I explained that she wasn't welcome in my place, and he promised not to let her in anymore.

You'd think that was the last I ever heard of her, but it wasn't. Eight years later, I got a call from a lawyer she'd hired. You know why? Because she was calling in that loan she'd given me for the trip. And she charged me for a bunch of other stuff she'd bought for me, too. It came to about fifteen hundred dollars.

It was easier to just pay the bill, rather than fight it. But that left a sour taste in my mouth. All that time had passed, and she finally decided to get back at me. To make me pay. All because she couldn't listen to me when we were together. Because she couldn't hear that I loved her. Because she had this idea in her head that she was afraid to let go of, that she was afraid was true.

It's just like my friend now who didn't believe me about my Morgellons. He didn't want to hear what I had to say because it upset his little world. It meant he had to change how he saw things. A few years from now, when everyone in the world knows about this Morgellons thing, and he can't avoid knowing I'm right, maybe he'll send me a bill, too. For all the fish hooks we lost over the years. Hooks, sinkers and fishing line.

I don't know if I'll still be around to pay that one.

Chapter 8
Harald

I was getting pretty fed up with this idea that the people around me thought I was crazy. Not everyone—my family's been really supportive—but some people. I felt as if I wasn't living my truth. As if I was hiding. And I didn't need that on top of the pain and feeling my confidence was down the tubes.

So I started spending more time online. Trying to connect with other people, learn about other Morgellons sufferers, keep working toward a cure. I mean, the Internet is how I found out about Morgellons in the first place. Where I learned about the magnetic bracelets that lifted the mental fog, where I discovered the borax wash, learned about drinking baking soda. And of course all those YouTube videos about chemtrails and smart dust and nanotechnology, too. It was the one place sufferers could really share information, and a lot of it was really helpful.

But none of that enlightened me the way Harald did. Finding Harald felt like fate. I thank God every day for Harald and what he taught me. He changed my life. He put all this suffering into perspective for me. He helped me see the real picture, the big picture of what's going on behind the scenes with Morgellons.

Harald's the real deal—a research scientist with an open mind. After the debacle of the CDC study, an open-minded approach was obviously necessary. Whether it was a cover-up, or the medical community failing to think outside the box, it definitely showed that a different way of looking at the world was needed. When I discovered Harald on YouTube, I discovered the last pieces of the puzzle that I needed to make sense of this whole Morgellons mess.

Harald Kautz-Vella does research all over the world, but his lab is based in Germany. If you want to hear him talk about Morgellons in detail, I've included the links to his YouTube talks at the back—they're with this British group called Bases at Woodsborough. But I'll summarize it for you, so you can understand why his research is so revolutionary for me.

First of all, his videos explain the chemtrails thing much more clearly than anything else I've seen. He shows images of an old Chemtrails course manual from the United States Air force Academy, proving once and for all that aircraft do, in fact, use chemicals in flight, for a whole variety of reasons—things like concealment, weaponry and other stuff, too.

Second, he showed some footage of Morgellons fibres floating under a back light out in the countryside, showing that they really do exist, that they really have infested many things other than human bodies.

Then, he explained how exactly nanotechnology can be incorporated inside a living body. He talked about a specific type of virus that takes over wasps. Their food supply is infected with these little bits of virus that then act inside the body of the wasp, essentially turning its brain off. This engineered "virus," which is really just a bit of nanotechnology, actually takes over the whole wasp and disrupts its ability to live like it normally would. Absolutely incredible.

Then Harald talks about this in relation to Morgellons, and he shows a Morgellons crystal that a patient shared with him. Under the micro-scope it keeps flashing blue at regular intervals—a pattern, a regular pattern like something manmade. But then, out of nowhere, it suddenly starts flashing red. It has been worked on in some way. Something else is controlling it. And Harald caught this all on camera, on footage attached to his microscope, and he shows it at his presentation. Man, when I saw that, especially after the story about the wasps—I got the chills big-time. I went cold all over. I suddenly realized how very, very sinister this is. It is big, and it is powerful, and it is evil. This "disease" that's in me, that's in every single living being on this planet, can be activated by some external source. It can turn human beings into who knows what. Let me tell you, that creeped me right out.

If all that wasn't enough, Harald starts talking about this alien substance that he's found and that he's been testing in his lab. And I say alien, because that's what he means. Alien, as in extra-terrestrial, as in from another world. It is creepy stuff, this stuff—it's sentient—it looks and acts like a strange little creature, but only when it thinks you're not watching. Otherwise, it's just a flat puddle of oily blackness. Seriously, I could not make this stuff up.

Anyway, this substance Harald has been testing—he simply calls it "black goo"—comes in two types. There's good stuff that the earth grows inside herself, and there's bad stuff—and that's the alien stuff. And the alien stuff is really old. Harald thinks it was shot into the world ages and ages ago—like eighty thousand years ago. So it is as old as or older than mankind. And that means it's been there since the very beginning, since the Garden of Eden.

Since the Garden of Eden. This corruption has been at the heart of the world for a long, long time. In fact, Harald believes that this black goo is at the heart of the corruption of mankind.

He explains how it's still working on the minds of the world's most powerful leaders. The sample of black goo that he has was collected from the Falkland Islands, and many of the most powerful people in the world—the Bush family, Angela Merkel—have secondary residences right on or about the place it has nested in the earth. To him, it's no surprise that governments under the control of these people have been making spurious decisions, because the influence this alien goo exerts is incredible. It promises power and wealth, just like the devil in the temptation of Christ, only most world leaders are not very Christ-like, and they give in. In return for vast personal wealth and personal power, they sell out the world. They compromise the very earth itself just so they can rule it for a short while.

All this sounds ridiculous, until you understand what this alien black goo is about. Essentially, it wants to subvert humans to host its parent alien species, which is really a version of artificial intelligence and not alive at all. So it is trying to take over the human race from the inside out, and Morgellons is its tool. Morgellons, that creepy little fibre that's not like anything else on earth, is alien. No wonder Morgellons fibres aren't like anything else! It's alien technology! Alien technology is living all over our world, inside life everywhere on the planet. And its spread has been encouraged and furthered by powerful members of high profile first-world governments—even if they don't know it—for the individual benefit of those people in power.

Now it all makes sense, doesn't it? All this strangeness, all these cover-ups, these fibres people can't identify—it's because this stuff isn't even made here on this earth. It's made outside this earth. And people who have the power to undermine this world and give it away for their own gain are happy to do that, because it makes their lives better, and they don't care about anything else. They won't be around to see the final destruction, so why should they care?

That sell-out attitude—people destroying other people's lives to pad their fortune and glorify themselves—might seem as if it only affects people at the top end of that ladder. People with enough temptation to bother. But look around you—it's infecting all of us, all the time. We care less and less about friends, and more and more about ourselves. And you know why? Because we care more and more about our technology.

We connect more with our technology than we do with real people now. How often do you actually sit down across the table from someone anymore, instead of talking to them on the phone? Or on Skype? Maybe you don't even talk. Maybe you just send them impersonal words: a text, an email.

And if you do sit down with a friend, how often is it in front of a computer? Or watching a TV show? Or, if you really are spending time face to face, how easily are you drawn away from it, by an incoming text, or a phone call, or an update on whatever your social media of choice is? Are you really even present? Or are you locked away in your own mind somewhere, hooked unconsciously into this vast network, waiting for another hit from the technology that's taken over your mind?

How often, when you do a Google search, do you type out the whole thing? Or do you pick from the suggestions Google gives you? What about when you write an email or a text on your phone? Do you pick the words offered to you? Do you actually say what you want, or do you pick words the phone suggests? How much of your life is now run by that thing in your hand? And how much do you worship it?

I see it all the time when I'm out and about: people moving their attention away from what's right in front of them so they can grab some electronic nugget of information that doesn't affect their lives in any material way. Like, at all. They just want to grab what's being fed into their minds. They want the satisfaction of it. And they can't stay focused on anything, can't listen to the people around them. Instead, they think their choices and their opinions and their viewpoints are the most important things in the world! How does that make sense? They can't focus for one minute but they think the world should offer them everything they want.

Well, it does, I guess. They can always get another hit from their phone. Because they're plugged in. That's all they're good for anymore. They've given up their humanity, their free will. And the leaders of the world have helped them do it. They did it first. They paved the way. And now this technology is infiltrating people's minds and bodies every day.

And you know what the worst part is? We all think it's progress. That we're getting somewhere. That something good is happening, that we're getting better. That all this technology is a blessing. Is it? Is it really?

You know, I remember a time when I could stand across the fence from my neighbour, and if he needed help with something, I'd help him. And if I needed help with something, he'd help me. And if something happened between us, like if a tree in my yard fell down on his fence, well, we'd figure out a way to deal with it together. We'd talk about it, and we'd both work at it, and side by side we'd figure it out. Nowadays, there would be lawyers and insurance companies and government and law enforcement all involved, all using their phones and computers to stick it to each other. We've gotten so we can't even look at each other, can't connect over the simplest things. How do we expect to solve any kind of crisis?

Now I see it. I understand this whole Morgellons thing is to blame. We're being taken over from the inside out. We don't even know it, and we can't stop it. We can't make a choice anymore—we're just plugged in all the time and we can't stop it. I mean, I run a business. I know what the world's like. Half my stuff at work is run through a computer now. I have to have email at work. I have to have a cell phone. My employees need to be able to get a hold of me when I'm away. I get it. I get how it works. But it makes me sick.

When did we come to accept this as normal? How did we agree to it? It's the most evil thing I can imagine, this fracturing away from each other. This choosing to be more concerned with ourselves than with each other. This refusal to engage with each other, to reach out and connect, however simply. But no, instead we each think our own small life is so damn important. We won't give it over for anyone. Even if someone stopped you and genuinely told you the secret for how to turn straw into gold, people would throw it away. They'd say, "I don't believe it," or "Now I have to change my life!" or "Why would you stop me? I'm busy! Can't you see I'm busy?" They wouldn't even hear it.

We don't stop to let things in anymore. We don't stop to think. Not unless we're getting that hit from our technology—then we'll let it do the thinking for us, decide how we should reply, put the words in our mouths. And remember, everyone tells us this is a good thing. The world is falling apart, and we're all celebrating.

Well, to me that proves one thing: This whole Morgellons mess really is driven from the top down by people who make choices only for themselves, and to hell with everybody else. They say good leaders lead by example, right? Well, if that's the case, they're doing a damn good job. They're ruining life for everyone below them, and after them. Leading by example. To me, that's enough proof that Harald is right—they've been promised the world by someone or something who doesn't have the right to give it. And we're all paying for their greed. We're all paying for their mistakes.

I mean, we know that. We know Eve was tempted by the devil. By something not human, something not of this earth. But that's where this whole thing started. With that temptation for knowledge. The devil's belief that knowing more can't hurt you. Well, we all know how that turned out. Cast out of Eden!

The most enlightening thing about all of this is how it was on the planet even before man. How this corruption has been in place since the first people, since Adam and Eve.

Now I'm somebody who believes what I was taught as a kid in church. I believe the Bible is true. You may not and that's okay. But I believe that what I was taught as a little kid is true: God made mankind. He made man in his image. He made Adam first, and then Eve, in the Garden of Eden.

Back then, the world as God made it was perfect. Everything was pure, unspoiled. The world was clean. It was holy. And Adam and Eve knew God, and they walked with him in the garden, and none of the animals fought–the lion lay down with the lamb, you know? That was the way life was supposed to be.

But then we messed it up. We messed it up because we disobeyed God. We did the one thing he told us not to. We looked at that tree in the garden, the tree of the knowledge of good and evil, and we said: "He's holding out on us, man! He's keeping the good stuff all for himself!" We wanted to taste it. We wanted to know. We've always got to push the limits; we couldn't just say, "This is what we're supposed to know, and that's what we're not supposed to know." No, we had to find out for ourselves.

And that was the original sin. Not trusting God. Thinking that knowing for ourselves was more important than trusting our creator. So Eve, helped by the serpent, was tempted, and she ate the apple. And then she gave it to Adam, and he ate the apple, too. And they both had their eyes opened.

And God came back to the garden, and he couldn't find them. And he looked all over, calling for them, calling their names, and finally he found them hiding. And he asked them, "Why are you hiding?" and they said "Because we're naked." And he asked, "How do you know you're naked?" even though he already knew. He already knew they'd eaten the apple, just like they weren't supposed to. But they told him, "Well, because we ate the apple. Even though you told us not to, God, we did anyway." And that was the end of that. They got kicked out of the garden, and they had to sweat and work and try to stay alive.

But we didn't learn, did we? We thought we knew better than God. But we didn't. And when we acted against what he told us, wanting to *know*, then we got into trouble. We used to live in paradise, then we had to work and slave for everything. Because we didn't listen. We didn't learn.

We still do that. We still push too hard, wanting to know things we've got no business knowing. We think knowledge is so important. We think we've got to learn more, do more, know more. The real truth is: *We aren't supposed to know. Knowing isn't always good.* But somehow we still think if we know more, then we'll figure out the secret and make our lives perfect again somehow.

So we keep building and building more things. We build up more knowledge, and we build up more technology, and we call it progress. But it's us still replaying that first sin over and over and over again. Every time we make new technology, claiming that this time we're going to know more, this time we're going to know everything—every time we do that, we're just playing into Satan's hands.

You know what I've come to realize? Technology is evil. Because knowledge is evil. Remember that whole eating from the tree of good and evil thing? Well, that's where we first went wrong. Because we didn't trust God's word. Instead, we decided we had to get more knowledge for ourselves. But the Bible expressly says the opposite. The Bible says, "Trust in the Lord with all your heart, and lean not on your own understanding." But we didn't do that. And now we've got this problem. We've got this idea that we have to know things, gather more and more knowledge, that there's an answer out there somewhere, a magic answer that can make everything better.

I'll tell you what I know. I know that we've done such a good job using technology that we forget to treat each other like human beings. We do such a good job building knowledge that we forget common sense. We don't believe our eyes unless something is "proven." And unless it's "proven" by "science," it can't be true. But remember: Common sense is common. It's available to everyone! Only it isn't so common these days, is it? We forget to use our own eyes and ears. We forget to pay attention to ourselves, to our own lives, to the people around us, the world around us. We ignore it. We take it for granted. But we expect it to just be there when we need it, to solve all our problems. Well I've got news for ya, folks! It ain't gonna be there! The world ain't gonna just be perfect and treat us great after we've done such a good job of not giving a damn.

You want to know how I know? I know because I see it in my face. We've infested the world with poison. We've blanketed it in nanotechnology. And I'm not talking about things like computers, or cellphones. I'm talking about smart dust—technology particles so small you can't even see them with your eyes. But they're there. Make no mistake. We've allowed tiny little technology particles to live and replicate and grow all on their own in the world. They even grow inside our bodies.

Learning about all of this, I just felt grief. Overwhelming grief. How could our whole world be such a disaster? How could we have known about this for so long and just ignored it? Because we did. We knew. We all knew about Adam and Eve. But we forgot.

All that thinking about Adam and Eve got me thinking about my own beginnings, about my own introduction to faith, to the Bible stories. I used to love the Bible stories. I remember, when I was a kid—probably six or seven—before we moved to the farm, anyway, I got this little ark for Christmas. Noah's ark, complete with all these little pairs of animals. Two by two they went into the ark. I loved that story, and I loved that toy. I played with it all the time. I even got a robe I'd dress up in to play it so I'd look just like Noah. I wanted to live out those stories for real.

In my own way, I was taught how. By our amazing Pastor Grandburg. He really was incredible. He knew how to reach everyone on their own terms. When I was pretty small, he helped me understand my faith in a whole new way. He helped me learn to face grief, and to face it like a good Christian, with my eyes always on Jesus Christ.

When I was three, we had this little dog—we just called him Puppy— and he was my best friend in the world. He and I did everything together. He'd sit beside me at dinner. He'd sleep on my bed. We were inseparable. That dog was everything.

He wasn't really mine, to begin with. He was the neighbour's dog, actually. But every day during the day, he'd come over into our yard and play with me and hang out. At the end of the day, when I'd go in for dinner, Puppy would just sit in the alley, outside the gate, waiting for me. Eventually Mom and Dad called over to the neighbours and asked if we could keep Puppy altogether. They were fine with that, and so Puppy became mine.

I had a lot of pride of ownership, even at that young age. We had a big yard, and in the back we each had a little garden plot. Each of us! When you're just a kid, three or four years old, having that sense of ownership is so important. That was my patch, and everything I grew in it was mine, and I was the one who made it grow! I had some amazing days back there, hanging out with Puppy, digging in my little garden. I can't remember what I grew. I don't think it was anything magnificent. But I loved it.

But the next summer, my beautiful little dog got run over. We were playing out by the street, and my mom had just called us in for dinner, when a big truck pulling a camper trailer came around the corner. And puppy was there in the street, and the wheel of the truck went right over him.

I didn't really get it at first. But Hellen did. Boy, did she set up a wailing. Such a noise! I never heard screaming like that before. She ran inside, shrieking and crying at the top of her lungs, saying something about Puppy—Puppy had been hit.

Mom and Dad came right out and into the street and went to the dog, and the guy got out of his truck, and was apologizing like crazy—he hadn't meant to hit him, he just hadn't known he was there. Anyway, Puppy was dead, all right. He'd died pretty much instantly.

It took a little while for that to sink in. But it left a big hole. I mean, that little dog and I did everything together. And now he wasn't there beside me when I fell asleep anymore. He wasn't there to play with me, or dig in my little garden.

The person who really helped me to understand it, to get past it, was Pastor Grandburg. He was just incredible—he didn't minimalize it, or treat me like a child. He just talked to me straight. He said he knew I was sad—of course I was sad! Puppy had been an awesome dog and an amazing friend. But the main thing he kept me focused on, the thing I could do to stop hurting so much was to put my hope in Jesus Christ. Jesus would get me through. Jesus was always with me, and he would never leave.

Poster Grandburg didn't lie about dogs going to heaven or anything. He didn't give me false comfort. I would've known it was false, anyway; I already had a sense that people were different from animals. That humans were special, somehow. That they alone would be called at the end of days. That didn't really bother me. I didn't need to have my puppy in heaven. I just needed to be treated like a grieving little boy, treated like a normal kid with real emotions. I needed to be respected in my own right, and guided. And Pastor Grandburg gave me that. And it really helped translate into a broader perspective as I grieved. He helped me put my focus where it belonged, with Jesus Christ.

All these years later, confronted with this horrific reality of how humans are fallen—how we've always been fallen—I am so, so thankful for my first teacher. My best teacher. The man who taught me how to live even through grief. The man who helped me understand what it meant to be a Christian, to keep my focus on God when times got tough. Especially when times got tough.

And you know what all that teaching has helped me to see? That this disease isn't just about alien technology. This is a disease of the spirit. It's the devil at work through Morgellons. He's trying to take away God's greatest creation: man. He's trying to turn man into something no longer alive. And he's using this alien technology to do it. It's been there since the very beginning. That alien black goo has been on this planet since Eden. It was there when the devil tempted Eve, and when she tempted Adam. It was Satan's tool. It's been his tool ever since.

The more I learn about this, the more I realize it's not only a physical battle I'm undertaking here. It's a spiritual one. Battling this, I am battling for my soul.

Chapter 9
Technology is Not Progress

We all come into this world alone, and we all die alone. My soul is here on a spiritual journey that only I can take. I get that. But sometimes I wish I didn't have to wake up and go to sleep alone, too.

One of the toughest parts of this whole journey with Morgellons has been facing it single. I mean, I do have support. I recognize that. I've got my mom. I've got friends. But I don't have one person who is willing to be there for me no matter what, who can stand by my side through thick and thin and comfort and support and love me through all this. Just as I would comfort and support and love her through whatever challenge she went through. I don't have a wife.

I haven't always been alone. I've had plenty of girlfriends along the way. But I never did find the one who was willing to stick with me through whatever life threw at us. Who was willing to put her love for me above all else, just as I would. I never did find that.

It isn't that I don't know how to be alone. I can spend time by myself. I know how to keep my own company. When I was panning for gold up north on my gold claim, I'd spend weeks at a time without seeing another living soul. Just me and the mosquitoes up there, except for the occasional trip into the Fort.

I was in between jobs—after I quit in Camrose, and before I started up with an optometrist, which was supposed to be in Whitecourt but ended up being in Wetaskiwin. Anyway, I had the whole summer off, and I'd bought some pretty basic gold-mining gear, and I went up north of Fort St. James and staked myself a gold claim back in the bush. And I spent May through August up there, most days by myself, sometimes spending a few days with my friends, Frank and Susan, or looking after their place while they went to see doctors in the city. But otherwise it was just me, down in the bush, working.

Funnily enough, I actually had a pretty serious girlfriend while I was up there. I'd be out in the river, running my sluice box, and I'd be thinking about her. I had this heart-shaped frying pan that she gave me that made wicked grilled cheese sandwiches and pancakes, so I got to be reminded of her every day, got to eat food made with her love even though she was miles away. It was pretty cool.

I had that pan and I had a journal, and I had a few pictures, but that was all the company I had. Day in, day out, I was alone. I'd get up and cook my own breakfast, and then work down by the river all day. I had this gravel bar that I'd work on, I called it the "mosquito bar," because my being on it made a blood bar for them. It did not matter how many layers of netting you wore, you'd get eaten alive.

No matter how well I'd seal up the trailer, they'd get in. Trying to sleep after an exhausting day, labouring all day hauling water and rocks, cooking your own food, doing your own cleanup, and having mosqui-toes buzzing around in your trailer ready to drink your blood all night long...that was horrible. Made it so hard to sleep, even though I was so exhausted. Even though my body was wrecked from having a log fall on me, and from pushing so hard day after day with sore ribs, in the cold and all alone. That was a challenge, that trip.

Funny how being alone like that is exhausting. How I'd think all day about food, and the next time I could justify heading back to the Fort to Skype with Laura. The panning was interesting—every time I'd see a fleck of gold in my pan my heart would leap—but I wasn't finding enough gold to feel it was something I could keep doing.

I lived on hope most days. Hope for a surprise the next day. Hope that my next tweak would help me strike it rich. Hope for a good meal at the end of the day. Hope for news from home. Hope for a visit with Laura. While I worked, long hours in the freezing cold water, driving the sluice box, panning and panning, I'd think about the future. I'd think about life. I didn't imagine I would end up like this. Sick. Struggling. Alone.

Things with Laura didn't work out. After I moved back to Alberta and got settled in Wetaskiwin, Laura and all three of her kids came to live with me. The two girls were in high school, and I didn't have super strong relationships with them. But her little boy was only four years old. And I remember spending some really great times with him. We'd make mud pies, and I taught him how to ride a bike, and we'd just hang out— messing around, playing, making up the world, the way kids do.

I distinctly remember one day that little boy was out riding his bike in the park, and we came back to the house, and he looked up at me, a big smile on his face, and said, "I love you, Steven." It just melted my heart. I'll never forget it—that open face, totally accepting, just full of love and joy. "*I love you, Steven.*" To have that kind of an impact on a little boy's life, to be a sort of father figure, to be there and just support him as he learns, as he figures out the world—that is one incredible gift. What an opportunity. What could I say to him, but, "I love you, too." And I meant it.

My mom really helped out with those kids, too. One time, Laura and I had planned a trip to Banff, and my mom came to stay at the house to look after the kids for the weekend. It was Easter, I think. Some long weekend in spring, anyway. We were supposed to leave on the Thursday morning, and my mom came up on the Wednesday night so all we had to do was load the car in the morning and hit the road. But then, when we woke up, it had snowed about a foot, and someone had broken the back windows of our car, so we had no rear window, and the inside was all soggy. We tried to get in touch with a rental car company and did end up getting a car and going away for the weekend, but it was one of those things. One of those signs, you know? Nothing's ever as easy as it seems it should be. Not where I'm concerned, anyway.

That was kind of the beginning of the end. I liked hanging out with her, but I also didn't feel as if she was contributing. As if she wanted to make a life together. I kept asking her to get a job, to find some work, anything. I didn't think I should be footing the bill for her and her family, when she wasn't doing anything but making the meals now and then. But she didn't think it was a problem. Oh, no. Eventually I gave her an ultimatum: Either you try and find work, or we're done. I'll give you a month.

She didn't, though. Didn't even write up a resume. Didn't even try. So after a month she moved back to her dad's house north of Edmonton. I remember the moving van broke down on her drive out there, and she called me up at nine o' clock at night, screaming into the phone, "The van's broken down, and isn't that just typical. Everything you touch is rotten. Rotten!" or some bullshit like that. So I called the moving company and got it sorted out. I thought that would be the last of it. It wasn't, though.

After about a month of living at her dad's she started calling me up, telling me how, oh, yes, she could get a job, thank you very much. She was bound and determined to show me that she was employable. As if somehow that would convince me to take her back. But nope. As far as I was concerned, it was too late for that. Too late. She had her chance. I gave her every opportunity, gave her time, everything. But she wasn't interested then. She couldn't see the value of what she had, not until it was taken away from her.

I wasn't going to accept that treatment. Either my partner valued me or she didn't. If she couldn't see me for who I was and what I was when we were first together, she wasn't the kind of person who would be able to stick it out. She wouldn't be there for me through thick and thin.

All my girlfriends seemed to leave and then to want me to take them back. Laura tried that, as did that girl in Calgary, and the girlfriend I had in Regina, too. They never knew how good they had it, I guess. Or they didn't realize they were throwing something valuable away.

Sally, the girlfriend I had in Regina, was probably the closest I ever came to making a life with someone. We were together for quite a while—moved in together and everything. We even tried to buy a house together. That didn't turn out too well, though. I should've known when that whole mess happened, that things weren't going to work out in the end.

We'd found this awesome little house—a small, old wartime house that had been recently fixed up and it looked so good—man, it looked great. We didn't have enough money for a down payment but the owner agreed we could do a rent-to-own sort of thing. We all got together, and he trusted us, said we seemed like nice folks, and we both had stable jobs and stuff. So we signed up for a rent-to-own on this perfect little house.

Well it was not so perfect, let me tell you. We hadn't been in that house more than a month before things started falling apart. The new hardwood hadn't been installed properly, so it started coming up everywhere. The paint was chipping on the walls. And the dishwasher overflowed and flooded the whole place. Anyway, it was a mess. So we moved out of there and into another apartment. But our relationship didn't last much longer, after that.

Remember how I used to go on those manager trips with the company? Well, one time, I had the most hellish trip back. I was leaving Mexico—I think we were in Puerto Vallarta that time—and the fire alarm went off while I was waiting to board the plane. The whole airport had to be evacuated and, of course, our flight was delayed. Then I missed the connecting flight in Los Angeles, and ugh, the whole thing was a mess. That should've been my first clue. When I got home the next day, almost twenty-four hours after I was supposed to, Sally picked me up at the airport, and everything seemed fine. She seemed happy to see me and all that.

But when we got home, she sat me down in the living room and gave me the Dear John letter. Said she'd started seeing someone else while I was away, and she was leaving me for him. Welcome home, Steven.

So I went out and got a nice new apartment all to myself. It was great, actually. It was on the first floor, by which I mean the first floor over the shops on the main floor. And it backed onto a massive deck that stretched out over the tops of the businesses underneath. It was huge, that deck, as big as my whole apartment again. It was great—I had plants out there and a hammock, a table and chairs—it was like my living room, especially in the summertime. Oh, I loved it. That's probably my favourite place I've ever lived, actually. Aside from my house now.

Anyway, it wasn't too long after we broke up that Sally tried to weasel her way back into my life. She tried everything, every trick in the book. Needed to use my washing machine. Needed to use my computer. Her TV wasn't working. Her phone line was down. I was nice to her, let her come and use my washing machine. We were friends. But there was no way I was letting her back into my life after what she did, cheating on me while I was away. Forget about it.

She loved that apartment. She'd come over all the time at first. And I'd let her in, and she'd do her laundry and we'd hang out, but that's all. She'd try and get me to let her stay over, but I wasn't having any of it. I knew better than to take her back. If I had, she'd have just broken my heart all over again.

Maybe it turned out for the best in the end. Can you imagine if I was married now? Do you think I could keep a wife, the state I'm in? I'm pretty sure she'd be gone. She'd have taken the kids and gone long ago, with me looking like this. That would be impossible to take right now — the love of my life, my life partner, walking out on me in my darkest hour. Not that I'd blame her. I've gotten pretty consumed by this thing. This disease. This infestation. It's serious stuff. How do you not get consumed by it? But how is that fair to anyone else in your life? Nope, most days I'm thankful I live alone. Sure, it'd be nice to come home to a hot meal once in a while, to not have to make it myself. But I'm realistic. I don't think anyone would really be able to stick with me through all this. I've got to do this alone.

It's been like that for most of the big things in my life. I've tackled them alone. I was alone when I started out on my vision path. I built my business alone. I bought my house alone. I'm used to it, now. And I've always had pets — fish and bird — some life in the place, something to look after, to keep coming home to.

And it's not as if I've isolated myself from the world. I've been in lots of people's homes, selling them stuff. I've lived in a lot of different places. All over the Prairies. I've seen a lot of different cultures and seen how different people live.

I'd thought I'd seen it all, actually. That was before I moved to Wetaskiwin. Working in Wetaskiwin was a real eye-opener for me. It's a really different culture there on the reserve. I mean, how they look at the world and how we do is very, very different. We think it's bad, and it's wrong, and, oh, how could they do these things to each other? But that's the way of life they know. It's pretty simple.

And we should take some responsibility for that. Our government should take responsibility for that. Ever since white man came here, they've been kicking the Natives around. They haven't been willing to listen. They haven't been willing to accept that maybe these people have a perfectly reasonable way of life. That maybe the Natives might have something to say about how we use the land that could benefit everybody. But oh, no, we've got to go on exploiting the land. Not looking after it. Oh no, that doesn't pay. We've got to make sure we scrape every dollar out of the land. We've got to get at that oil. And if that walks all over Native rights, well then, they should just get good honest jobs and stop complaining. But, I mean, look what we did to them.

Anyway, it's very different there, on the reserve. I remember this one guy came into the shop with an oxygen tank and an oxygen mask. He wasn't very old, maybe in his fifties, if that. I figured he must be really, really sick, being on oxygen and everything. But no, turned out his wife had stabbed him in the chest and punctured his lung. And I mean that was normal. Well, not normal, but I saw a lot of casual violence like that. People just didn't think anything of it.

I remember a week later that same guy—let's call him Jack—came in asking for a sunglasses clip, because he'd lost his. So I looked him up in the system and found out what kind of glasses he had, and discovered we had one more clip I could sell to him. So I sold it to him for twenty-five bucks or whatever. Then a couple of days later, Jack called me up and told me he found his clip, and asked if I would be willing to take the other one back. I tried to talk him out of it, saying having a second one might be handy to have in the car, or in case he lost the first one again. But he really wanted me to take it back, so I said, all right, come on down, and you can return it.

So he came down to the store and brought the clip back. It still looked like new and everything so I returned his twenty-five bucks. Then the next day, I was opening the store and my colleague said to me, "Hey, did you hear about Jack?" And I said, "No, what?" It turned out he'd overdosed on cocaine and died the night before.

That one really stuck with me. Was the extra cash he'd gotten from me by returning that clip the reason he overdosed? What if I'd never let him return it, would he still be alive? That ate at me for days.

I used to have feelings of guilt like that growing up, too. When I was in high school, there was this one big kid, Charlie, who just loved to pick on me. He always insisted we fight.

Now, I hate fighting. I don't trust myself not to injure someone. I feel the tiniest bit of pain and I just lose it. And I don't know how I'd live with myself if I really did injure someone—if I broke a bone or damaged a brain—or worse, if I killed somebody. I couldn't do it. I couldn't bring myself to fight. I've only had a real fist fight maybe twice in my life. I avoid them like the plague.

Anyway, this guy, Charlie, kept egging me on, looking for a fight. I'd always turn him down, get in my truck and leave, whatever. But this one night, we were at a party and he just came out of nowhere and jumped me from behind, jumped on me and started punching me in the back of the head.

I just turtled. I didn't want to fight. But he kept hitting me and hitting me until eventually some guys pulled him off and sent him on his way.

Well, can I tell you? I didn't feel too warmly towards him after that. I wished all manner of bad luck on him. I wished he'd break his hand, or get in a car accident. I told my friend Ted I wished Charlie would die.

Well, not long after he'd beaten me up, Charlie got in a canoeing accident. He was out alone in his canoe, and he drowned.

When I heard about it, I felt so sick. Guilty sick. All nauseous and sweaty. I had wished this man ill, and then he had died.

Ted called me on it, too. He stopped my truck in the middle of the road—blocked the street with his car, got out and stormed over to me. "It's your fault, Steve. You wanted him dead, and now look what happened. You better not wish anything bad on me." Then he sucker-punched me in the face and took off.

I was in total shock. What on earth had just happened? I did wish something bad on him—I was so angry that he was making me feel guilty for Charlie dying. And not long after that, Ted got in an accident and was crippled. He could never walk again. And his brother died of cancer, too. And the first guy I ever fought with in school died really young as well.

That stuff starts to pile up after a while. You wonder whether it's all just coincidence, or whether you really do have that kind of power.

Mostly I just started to watch my thoughts. I promised not to wish harm on anyone ever again.

But with Jack, in Wetaskiwin, it wasn't something I'd thought about. It was something I'd done. It took me a long time to come to terms with it. I talked to my mom about it, and she pointed out that it wasn't me who went and bought the cocaine for him. It wasn't me that put it up his nose—he did that. Jack made those decisions for himself.

Eventually, I was able to realize that I can only be responsible for my own actions in this world. For my own choices. I can't choose for anyone else. Each of us has got to make that choice for ourselves. Doesn't mean it's easy. Doesn't mean people always choose right. And we can stand up for each other where we can, and all that. But it wasn't up to me to choose for Jack. I could never have done that. It was he who made the decisions that led to his death.

That's a hard lesson to learn. It took me a long time to get there. Because I really believe in helping people. Communities should help each other, you know? But I can only do so much. Other people have to be accountable for their selves. There's nothing I can do about that.

One of the good things that came out of Wetaskiwin was I started racing cars at the Edmonton raceway. I first went with a guy from work on a Saturday when we weren't working, And it was pretty cool, seeing all those cars whipping around the track. But I thought it'd be even cooler to be down there driving.

So I went and I found a car and I brought it down to the track and I started racing. I did okay at first, middle of the pack or so. But then I met this guy who was a mechanic, a specialist at tuning engines and stuff. And he gave me a lot of pointers about how to get the most out of my car. I listened really close and took notes, and then I went home and did everything he said. And did it make a difference! I started doing really well, top-three finishes most of the time, when I wasn't winning.

I remember this one race, it was the feature race of the day, the big one, and I was in the lead. We were on the last lap of the race, and this other driver was behind me, and I knew he was going to try to overtake me on the last corner. So I just positioned the car so he couldn't really get around me. Well, he didn't like that. Not one little bit. He tried to take me out of the race, went up high on the side and came down right into my back quarter panel, trying to take my car out. Well, he turned me around all right. I ended up crossing the finish line backwards. But I was still in the lead! I won that race, even going backwards. And I was able to pull out of the spin and drive the victory lap. After the races, we'd always have fans down into the paddock to come see the cars and take pictures with the drivers and stuff. And there was this one boy of about seven who couldn't wait to come meet me and see my car that day. His mom said he was so excited, he couldn't believe he was going to meet the best driver at the track. He looked up at me, and he said, "I know you must be the best driver here, mister, because you won that race, even going backwards!"

It was a bit of a tradition we had to get the kids to sign our cars. You should've seen his face light up when I handed him a gold Sharpie and asked if he wanted to sign my car. He was just beaming. He put his name on the car, right above the wheel on that back quarter-panel. I thought that was fitting.

Winning was great, and racing was a lot of fun. But not everyone appreciated that I was doing so well. I came to the track one day, hours before the races, and found the hood of my car all dented. I opened it up, and someone had pulled out all the wires, disconnected the spark plugs, tampered with the engine and such. Petty sabotage. I managed to get everything back together and was able to race, but I just felt this nauseous feeling in my gut. Seriously, who does that? Well, I know exactly who did it. But I mean, really? C'mon. If you want to beat me, find a way to beat me honestly. Just taking me out of the race doesn't make you a better driver than me, and we both know it.

After that little incident I started locking up my hood on the car when I was away. I didn't have a garage to keep it in, so I kept the hood locked, and that seemed to help. I didn't have any more issues for a while. But then, a little later—I was starting up my eyewear business at this point—I came to the track to find my locks cut. I opened the hood and looked at everything, and it all seemed okay, so I decided to go ahead and race that day. I started the car and pulled up to the line, but even in the first race I could tell something was off. I didn't have the usual power. But I pushed through. I finished the race. I ran the next one, too. But about halfway through the third race—the feature race—my car just died. And I mean died. I couldn't get anything out of it at all. Nothing. I got it towed to the garage, and we realized that someone had dumped a bunch of metal filings into my oil, and the whole engine was ruined. The car was bust! I was so, so choked about that. I loved that car.

I did get another car. And it did okay, but it wasn't the same. Then I got a bigger car and went up a race class. But I was just doing okay, and besides, by that time I had my business going.

With the store and the move to Red Deer, racing got a lot harder. I'd have to leave the store at four o' clock sharp on Saturdays and head straight to the track, and even then I'd roll up just minutes before the races were due to start. And sometimes that was okay. But sometimes it wasn't—I wouldn't be in the best head space, wasn't very focused, so I wouldn't race as well. And then all that sabotage happened with my car. Showing up and not knowing if your car's been messed with, and not having any time to put it right—I hated going out to the track and not knowing what I was going to get.

After my car got busted, it just wasn't the same. I had the new car, but the real thrill of it was gone. I didn't want to just do it for fun. If I was going to do it, I wanted to win. So I didn't race for that much longer after Eyewear got up and running.

I did get a little '53 Chevy, though—a little two-door, hard top, tool-around sort of car. After I bought it, I got it all fixed up. I had to do a bunch of the work myself, and some things I hired a mechanic friend of mine to do. It took a couple of years, but we got it all done. It's a beautiful car, my Sunday driver. I take it out for a leisurely tool around town. Just go for a drive, you know? No destination in particular, just enjoying being behind the wheel.

And then I got the Hummer for business advertising. That's the one I put the eyewear sign on. A big black Hummer with simple gold lettering—it's pretty eye-catching. I've had two of those. I got the first one in 2006, then traded it in for a newer one in 2010. And then there's the truck for out on the acreage. And I've got a few other cars bombing around in storage, in my garage at the house. Don't have the same time for them, though, these days. I've sold off a couple. Might as well, then someone else can enjoy them. No sense in a car sitting around and not getting used. They're not made to look at.

I still love cars. I've spent a good many hours working on cars with friends. Hanging out and tinkering, having a few laughs. I made a few friends because of the racing stuff. But in the end, all that stuff with the race cars was just a distraction. It was something fun to do. It gave me something to do and something to shoot toward. But it didn't stay. It didn't fill any hole in my life. Cars are great, and I love them, but they're just cars.

I'm glad I did it. I hated how it ended, though. Whenever I think about that guy wrecking my car, just so he could beat me — it makes me so sad. Why do we have to drag others down to make ourselves feel better? I'll never understand that. Why can't we just push, and try, and be the best we can be?

Can I tell you? Nothing makes me madder than people betraying other people, betraying their responsibilities to others. I believe we owe something to each other. We share a planet. We share a world. We share a community. But people forget. They get so hollow, or empty, or rotted inside, that they need to cut you down. When they cut you down they feel better, more powerful, more in control. But in the end nothing can ever make them powerful enough. And that's why we've got this whole Morgellons mess in the first place. I shouldn't be surprised. It's been with us since the beginning. Since Adam and Eve. Since The Fall. People keep undermining each other. When will we learn to start having real conversations again, reach out for real solutions? I've begun to feel like that day will never come. Not now. Not with Morgellons. Not with technology taking over the world the way it is. It's too late. We didn't wake up soon enough, and now it's too late. I don't have any hope left for the world.

Chapter 10
I Live in Hell

When I was a kid, I used to get this dream. A nightmare, really, the way I experienced it. In this dream, I'd see this tiny little fuzz ball, kind of like a round speck of lint. And in my dream, I was associated with this little ball somehow. I knew that in the dream that ball of fuzz represented me.

Always in the dream, I would be that little ball of fuzz, and I'd be watching this gigantic ball of fuzz roll toward me. It was kind of like me, that gigantic ball of fuzz, only it was way, way, way bigger. It totally dwarfed me. And every time, it would roll straight toward me until it rolled right over me and I was gobbled up by that great big ball of fuzz. Subsumed by it. And once I got gobbled up by the big ball of fuzz, I couldn't identify with that little bit of fuzz anymore. It was as if whatever it was that made me *me*—whatever made me a unique individual who mattered in the world—had just disappeared. Been swallowed up. Consumed.

I'd wake up in a cold sweat every time I had that dream. Just soaked. It was so terrifying. I know it sounds silly—a little ball of fuzz gets rolled over by a big ball of fuzz, so what? But it was so vivid and real. To just be erased like that, to be swallowed whole...it was terrible. It was so raw and visceral. I felt as if I was being erased.

I had that dream for years. It started when I was probably about five and continued until I was maybe twelve or thirteen. I remember the last time I had it, it was just as terrifying as the first time. I woke up in the middle of the night, completely terrified, and couldn't go back to sleep. Eventually, I went and crawled into my parents' bed. I was so embarrassed—here I was, practically a teenager, and I was sleeping in my parents' bed because of a nightmare. But I was crawling out of my skin with fear, and that was the only thing that could get me back to sleep.

The implications these days are not lost on me. My self, my being, is being swallowed up by this alien force. I am being taken over. I wonder, sometimes, is something inside of me being overwritten? Am I being erased, somehow? Am I losing myself and I don't even know it?

Maybe that's the root of all this mental fog. Maybe I feel groggy and out of sorts and fuzzy in my mind because I'm slowly losing myself. It was better there for a while. It's worse again. Not as bad as before, but worse than it was. I've got magnetic bracelets around my ankles now. And my wrists. I'll do anything. I'll do whatever it takes.

One of the things I keep thinking about is the Dead Sea. I've been thinking a lot about how Morgellons has infiltrated the whole world. And it got me wondering if there's any place on earth where there's no Morgellons, where Morgellons can't live. I'm looking for hope, see. I'm looking for some resistance, somewhere on earth.

Anyway, I thought of the Dead Sea. After all, it's called the Dead Sea because nothing can live in it. Because it's so salty, so alkaline. And I started to wonder, what if Morgellons can't live in the Dead Sea, either? What if going there, I could for once be in a place where there are no new Morgellons getting inside of me? Maybe that's what I need to get a jumpstart on this thing.

Somewhere, somehow, the little gears were turning in my mind, and I realized that what I had been doing with my regime was making my body like the Dead Sea. Making it so Morgellons doesn't want to live in me anymore. I mean that's the whole point of the baking soda. It helps make the body more alkaline. Makes my body a place Morgellons is less likely to live. Makes it want to get out.

It's been months now since I first started this regime: the bracelets, the borax, the baking soda. I thought it would only be a month or so, and then I'd be healed. But no. I keep moving forward, slowly. But it's almost as if I take one step forward and two steps back. The lesions are creeping down my arms again. They're creeping onto my chest.

I keep telling myself that I'm getting more lesions because what I'm doing is working. I'm making my body uninhabitable to them. So of course, that is followed up with a fresh eruption of lesions. All these little fibres in my skin, they have to go someplace. They want to get out, out, out. Because I'm making my body uninhabitable for them.

So I should be celebrating. I'm getting somewhere. It's just hard to get excited about another round of this. Great. Just great. A fresh round of pain. Yee-haw.

Do you know how exhausting it is? Pulling little fibres, little electronic gizmos out of your skin? Do you know what it's like, picking bits of nanotechnology out of your body? I never stop being disgusted by it. It never stops making me angry. It's not right. It's not natural. In fact, it's diabolical. It's evil working inside me, trying to take over my body. No wonder it hurts so much. These little bits of computer are trying to integrate themselves into my being. When I pull them out, I'm tearing myself open.

But I have to tear them out. I'm tearing them out, ripping open my skin, so that I can heal it. It's the only way. Get them out.

It's funny, though. My skin wants them out, too. It heals over super quickly when I finally get the fibres out. I can always feel when another lesion is starting up. It's like a burrowing, something digging out of my skin. So I spray a baking soda solution over the spot, and I keep misting it until it's good and wet, until the skin starts to show this biofilm. And that's the sign that it's nearly ready.

When I notice that biofilm, I start rubbing the spot—really gently, with just the lightest amount of pressure. But I keep rubbing at it, back and forth, gently. Keeping it wet with the baking soda. And then eventually it erupts. The biofilm peels back, and whatever's underneath it spews out in a hiss of angry purulent gunk, with the hard little crystal-like bits inside it. And, wow, does that hurt. When it finally bursts it's the most painful thing, stinging and stinging almost as if you've burned yourself. - It's white-hot like that.

But then half an hour later, the skin's covered over, and it looks almost normal. You'd never know this eruption of goo just exploded out of it thirty minutes ago. It's surreal.

This whole thing is like being in a brand new world. I don't recognize the world around me anymore. It's alien. Forbidding. Unhappy. I wish I could escape it, sometimes. I have this feeling that I just want to go home, to be safe, to rest. But I can't.

Everything's different. Everything's hard. I feel as if I'm living in a foreign land, where I know all these things inside myself, but everyone keeps looking at me funny. As though they can't understand me.

I guess they can't.

That feeling—that discomfort, disassociation almost—it doesn't take long for it to settle into a feeling of grief. Loss. As if I've been cast out from my world.

I've felt like that before. When I was a kid, moving from the city to the farm. Yeah, sure, it was exciting in some ways—I was looking forward to the animals and all that. But when the move came, I really started to feel that sense of loss.

Back in Calgary, I had neighbourhood friends. We'd play kick the can in the street every night, until the light faded. Out on the farm there was no one to play with. My nearest friend lived a mile away, not right across the street or the back alley like in Calgary. We couldn't gather a bunch of kids for kick the can. And even if we could, they wouldn't understand it, anyway.

It wasn't that bad for me. I was only eight. And when you're eight, you don't really know any better. It's just what is. You take what's handed to you because you just don't know any better. You adapt. You adjust, easier than older people do. I know, because that move was pretty rough on my sister Hellen.

Hellen was thirteen when we moved, a teenager. And teenage girls are nasty. She got teased mercilessly. She got spit on and bullied nearly every day at school. She'd come home in tears. She had it way rougher than I did.

Being in school was tough for me, too, though. Every one of my classmates had known each other for years. All their lives. They'd started school together, and they'd had years to get to know each other already.

It may not seem like a lot, only two or three years, but it was an eternity, especially when you're eight. And kids can smell an outsider. They're great at picking up on differences. They make you feel it. They knew I wasn't one of them, and they made sure I knew it, too.

That's an experience you never forget, being the outsider. I was always sure to make friends with the new kids after that. I knew what it was like not to see a friendly face in the halls. So whenever a new kid came to town after that, I'd always say hi, get to know them, smile at them in the halls.

I wish there were someone looking out for me like that now.

It's not even the loss as much As it is the violation. Someone—something has invited itself into my world, into my house, into my being. It's intolerable. It's unendurable. I don't think it's something you can ever prepare for. I don't think it's something you really recover from, either. It shakes your trust. It makes the whole world a little bit darker.

Back when I was living up in Fort St. John in northern B.C., I took a trip to Edmonton to finish a course for my optician's diploma. While I was gone, one of my friends broke into my place. He didn't literally break in, but somehow he'd filched my house key and had a replica made, and he used it to get into my apartment while I was gone.

When I got home, I walked into a total mess—it was like a war zone. There was crap everywhere. Like, literal crap. And they'd destroyed the place—broken my furniture, punched holes in the wall. And they hadn't confined themselves to my apartment, either. The building super had complaints because people had used the stairwells like a bathroom. There was vomit dripping down the railings. He'd even used my car—I'd grabbed a cab to the airport, so my keys were in my place—and he got a DUI while he was driving it around.

I've never felt so violated in my whole life. It was the worst betrayal. After that experience, I couldn't feel good in my own skin for such a long time. So much of my trust was shattered—in myself, in other people. How could I have misjudged someone so badly? How could someone have thought it was okay to act like that? Treat someone else's stuff like that?

Anyway, I had to move home after that. I tried living somewhere else in Fort St. John—I had a really good job up there, and I had an amazing boss. But I couldn't do it. I just felt so, so violated. I had to move back home. I had to surround myself with people who cared about me. It was such a kick in the nuts.

But back then, I could leave it. I could move away. There's no getting away from this. From the now. The mess of my face. The mess of Morgellons. There's no hiding. There's no relief.

At least I have my house. At least I have something stable. This house is the first place I've ever owned. Everywhere I was before, I always knew it was temporary, that I wasn't going to be there forever so there was no point in settling down. Except that one time in Regina, but fate intervened on that one.

But yeah, I've been in my place almost ten years now. About a year and a half after my store managed to get off the ground, I was doing so well that I figured I could buy a house. So I went to the bank, and started looking around for a place. And I found this little acreage just out of town. It was perfect. Great location, easy to get in and out, lots of space, nice and private. Plus the house had everything I wanted: garage, deck, big yard with an orchard, the whole bit.

Well, I'd just settled on the house, when one day this guy came into the store. He was talking on his phone to a friend, and he said, "No, man, it just sold!"

Anyway, I asked him about it, what had happened. And he started telling me about this gorgeous house he'd seen on an acreage just out of town, and he'd just called his Realtor to put an offer on it and found out it only just sold. "Man, it was the perfect little house! It had all the stuff—the garage, deck, a great location—everything!"

I said, "I agree with you. Sorry, man. Hate to tell ya, but it was me who bought it."

"Well, what did you get it for?"

I told him. And then he offered me a hundred thousand dollars more for it, right there. Can you believe that?

I turned him down, though. I mean, what was I going to do with the extra cash? And I'd be stuck looking again. Besides, this little house is perfect. It's got everything I've ever wanted.

I've done some work to it since. Built a fence, did some renovations, built my gazebo. I've got a whole menagerie here, too. I've got rabbits and squirrels—I get a ton of wildlife through here.

Which is not always a good thing, mind you. I had this pet rabbit in the backyard, in this caged off little piece of wilderness I built for it. One day, I was out sitting on the deck, and this massive owl—the biggest owl I've ever seen—just swooped down out of nowhere, picked up that rabbit and carried him away. It's the cycle of life, I guess. But I never enjoy seeing something that's close to me snatched away like that. It feels ugly. It feels vindictive, somehow, as if life has no empathy.

Maybe it doesn't. Maybe only humans have empathy. Maybe that's really what sets us apart. Maybe empathy is a function of soul.

Empathy's not the same as forgiveness. But forgiveness is important, too. Even if that's a hard one to learn. And it takes more than just words.

When I was maybe six or seven, my sister and I built a snowman in the backyard in Calgary. It was a big one—bigger than she was, even. We had to climb up on to the trampoline to put the head on, that's how big it was. I think my dad helped; I can't remember. We put the carrot nose in, and buttons for the eyes—everything. And I just remember being so proud of it.

We came home from school a day or two later to find the snowman kicked over. Some kids—older kids, teenagers most likely—had come into our yard and knocked down our snowman! And to top it off, they'd slashed the trampoline, too, slit it right down the middle with a knife. I was devastated. Who does that? Who is so small and mean that they have to go into another person's yard and destroy their stuff? I really just didn't understand it. That hurt a lot.

That was my first lesson in forgiveness. It was a good lesson, too. I knew that it was up to me to forgive their meanness. That was my responsibility. But it was hard.

I remember I used to have these dreams as a kid where I was flying— up above the world looking down on it as if from an airplane. I loved the idea of it. I thought flying was the best. And the dreams felt really real, too. Because every now and again, I'd have this sensation of falling, as if I was tumbling headlong out of the sky, and I'd jerk awake in my bed, but the bed would be shaking, as if I really had fallen from a great height.

Anyway, after that incident with the trampoline and the snowman, I'd be having my flying dream, and I'd imagine that I was flying over Calgary, looking for those kids who ruined my stuff. In my dream, I'd know that I was about to find them and punish them.

It got complicated, though. I knew about bombs and guns and stuff by then. I remember that in my dream I'd be thinking: I'm going to drop bombs on you monsters. And then I'd wake up with my bed shaking as if I'd just been dumped into it. It was terrifying. I knew it was bad to drop bombs on people—that's probably what woke me—but in my dream I just wanted to punish them for hurting me like that. I still hadn't forgiven them, not really, not in my heart, even though I said I had.

And I didn't like it. I didn't like being vindictive like that. It made me really uncomfortable that I wanted to hurt these people who had hurt me. I knew I should rise above that. I knew I ought to be able to forgive.

But forgiveness is hard. Empathy is even harder. I don't think you can really have empathy until you experience something. Until you have to go through pain and suffering and struggle. Then you can hear where other people are at. That's when you value kindness.

No one values kindness anymore. No one values empathy. The world is just so lost, so focused on me, me, me. Wrapped up in ourselves. Wrapped up in our technology. We don't even talk about kindness anymore. We've forgotten we even used to care.

It's hell.

I am living in hell.

I know that now. It's not something I take lightly. I don't mean to be melodramatic. But I am.

All around me I see people who don't care. Who can't be bothered to listen. Who can't stop looking at their cellphones long enough to see the life around them. It tears me up inside. It makes me ache with pain. And that's on top of the physical burden. I am aching inside and out.

Every single day is filled with pain. It's damn near unendurable. It's not, obviously. I'm here; I'm alive. I'm enduring. But it's the most difficult thing I've ever done. Every day I fight layers of judgment. Layers of apathy. And that's on top of this disease.

I'm battling. I'm in it. I'm alive. But it's as if every single moment of every single day is the most difficult one I've ever lived. If that sounds exhausting, it is. If it sounds difficult, let me tell you: It is. It's incredibly hard. I'd say it's impossible. But it's not. There you have it: a paradox. I am enduring the unendurable. I am surviving the impossible. Somehow. But it really is like living in hell.

One thing I don't feel cut off from is God. On the contrary, communing with God is the only thing keeping me alive. I think if I didn't have faith, if I didn't have an understanding that killing myself would cut me off from God forever, I'd have done it a long time ago. My faith, Jesus Christ and God are the things keeping me going, keeping me alive. Because what's the point of trying to escape hell by killing myself if all it does is put me right back in hell? And what if it's *worse*? And it would be worse—I'd be cut off from God, for real, in hell. I'd be cut off from any shred of love or relief. And that would entirely defeat the point of living.

I've made it sound as if I'm using God. I'm not. I think I'm closer to God than I've ever been. That sounds stupid; God is supposed to be about love, not suffering. God is supposed to be about forgiveness and redemption, not pain and more pain. But I'll tell you something. The more pain I've experienced, and the more impossibly difficult it's become to do basic things like eat and sleep, the more I need a reminder that I'm more than human. That the flesh is just one part of my being—that I'm more than these sensations of pain streaming into my mind. That I am a spiritual being. And as I've grown in awareness of that—as I've been able to lose my pain in contemplation of God—I've been filled with this feeling of holiness. I've found myself filling up with God's blessings of love.

I know, I said just a minute ago that I was living in hell. Now I'm telling you that I'm full of God's love. I sound like a crazy person, don't I? But here's the thing: Both of these things feel true. I am tugged in both these directions all the time. All the time. My body is in hell, and my heart is with God, and I'm torn in two and I feel as if I could explode at any given moment.

I've been trying to stay away from technology. I keep my phone in an old coffee jar, full of dried beans with the lid on. I don't want to look at it. I don't want to hear it. Every now and then I pull it out, just to check what's going on. Just to check whether my worldly ties are calling. Mostly they're not. Mostly I just sit and pray, or work on my face, or cry.

I do spend a lot of time working on my face. I soak it in borax or baking soda and rub at the biofilm, try to peel it off so the sores can be open to the air. They have a better chance to heal that way, and the Morgellons fibres come out more easily. But that biofilm is nasty stuff. It doesn't want to come away. So I sit with a cloth drenched in baking soda wash and my spray bottle, and I keep the skin moist enough to rub the film away. Sometimes this takes hours. And it's painful. But I try to do it every day. I want this thing gone. I'll do everything I need to. I won't leave any stone unturned.

Another thing I've been doing a lot—and in some ways this is easier— is I make baking soda or borax baths. They work great. I pour most of a box of borax or baking soda in the tub, and then I sit in there for a couple of hours and let the baking soda do the work. It gets into the lesions under the water and they get all soaked in there, as if they're in the Dead Sea. And I can sit in the bath and pray, and let the tears just flow, and forget for a little while that I'm living in hell. It's the best relief I find anymore. I just have to watch I don't fall asleep.

Sleep is something that's hard. Like, really impossible. However I lie, I hurt. My arms hurt, or my chest hurts, or my back hurts. The lesions at my temples hurt. And I'm either too cold or too hot, and I get the chills and that hurts. And while I'm lying there, staring at the darkness, that's when the devil gets his way.

I know he's watching me. He's watching me all the time. I see it. The other night, I was trying to sleep, and I just had the sense that he was up there, staring down at me from the sky, watching. Waiting for me to give up, to cave in. It got so I couldn't stand it. You know that feeling that something or someone is watching you? Well, knowing what I know about Morgellons, I was pretty sure that was true. I mean, I don't have any electronics in my room at all. None. Not even an alarm clock, anymore. At least not a digital one. I've got one of those wind-up mechanical ones; it works just fine, and I don't feel as if anyone's spying on me while I'm sleeping.

But anyway, this other night I couldn't get to sleep. I just knew—I *knew*—that someone was watching me. So, I thought, okay, I've got to figure out what this is. I climbed out of bed, put my bathrobe on, went outside and looked up at the sky. And what do you know? There was this thing moving in the sky—big, grey and low—with little lights on it. And I just froze, staring up at it, thinking: *Oh my God, this is it—there's an alien spaceship. Satan really is spying on me. He really is looking down on me, using all this alien technology to check up on how I'm doing. I've turned everything off, and I'm foiling his plans, so he has to come look at me himself.*

I knew no one was going to believe me, so I wanted to film it. I ran inside for my video camera, but by the time I got back out there, the sky was clear again. It was gone. I waited for a bit, just to be sure, but I didn't see anything else weird. At least not that night, anyway. So I went back to sleep. And I didn't have the feeling of being watched anymore, so I guess I scared him away. I guess he didn't want to be noticed or something.

Anyway, you'd think sleep would've come easily. But it didn't.

Chapter 11
I Will Not Kill Myself

I'm not the only person who finds this disease unendurable. Debilitating. Diabolical. So many people have killed themselves over this disease. Can you blame them? The pain and the horror of it—it's intense. It's so hard. It really is impossible to bear. And no one helps us. No one believes our pain, listens to our experiences, anything. The world denies us our dignity. Refuses us healthcare, disability leave. Tells us we're crazy. We get thrown under the bus while we're screaming for help. It's no wonder some people can't handle it. It's no wonder they take their lives.

Some days I don't think I can handle it, either. I can't imagine anyone being able to endure this for long. It's been, what? Eight months for me since I knew what this was? Maybe five since it got bad? It's gotten worse since I've tried to drive it out. My body's rejecting it more strongly than ever. And it drags me down.

I think about it; I won't lie. Sometimes I think it'd be easier. Just end it. End this life. End this pain. Get out. Kill myself. Commit suicide.

I won't.

I know I won't.

I won't give up that easily.

Remember that day when I first discovered Morgellons? That day that kicked all this craziness off? When I was out in my yard, praying to my

Lord and Saviour, Jesus Christ, on my knees in the rain, asking how I could do his will, when I looked like this? And how I had this powerful sense that *I was going to get to the bottom of this?*

Well, that day, when I saw all those photos of people's lesions, the fibres and crystals they pulled out of their skin, when I read all those descriptions and testimonials from these people who were quite sure that they were dealing with something unexplained, something that was very, very serious —

That's when I knew.

That's the day I had my epiphany: My purpose on this earth wasn't something I was going to fulfil after I cured this infection. The infection *was* my purpose on this earth. I hadn't wanted to see it. It was ugly and hard, and uncomfortable and scary. I didn't like it. But it was my purpose all the same. God had called me to be the person who brought Morgellons to the world.

It came like a stroke of lightning that day, obvious and startling and blinding in its clarity.

I remember sitting in front of my computer screen and trembling, awed and terrified and overwhelmed by the awful hideousness of this disease laid out on those pages for me, shaking with the realization that *this was it. This was my purpose. Living with this thing, beating this thing was my purpose.*

I knew I had to act. I mean, when something that big hits you, you do something. At first I thought it meant making a start towards a cure. It's only lately that I've realized it's much, much bigger than that.

I mean, you know by now how huge this disease is. Even calling it a disease doesn't do it justice. At all. It's so much more than a disease! It's a corruption of this whole world. It's a spiritual corruption that's rotting the world as we know it. A spiritual corruption with physical manifestation. A disease? Yeah, a disease of humanity, a rot of the soul.

The more I learned, the more I realized that Morgellons is really serious stuff. That it's truly diabolical — it's of the devil, in the truest sense of the word. And the more I realized that, the more I realized just what exactly I was being called to do.

My God has chosen a massive task for me. I always knew I was put on this earth for a special purpose. I always knew that. But I never, ever imagined it would be this huge.

Or that it would be this hard.

I keep coming back to thinking about Pastor Grandburg. About how he gave his whole life to God. He never had a wife. He was never married. He was always alone, just like I am. Except he was never really alone, because he had God. He was kind of married to God in a way. Married to the church. That was the true love of his life, and he wasn't going to divide up his love and attention by having a family, too. And I bet that was hard sometimes. Sometimes you just want love, contact—a heartfelt connection with another human being. Well, he never had that. Not in a marriage kind of way.

I'm trying to do like Pastor Grandburg taught me and keep my focus on Christ. Keep my focus on the good things I've got, the things I'm thankful for. And remember that, like him, I've been called. He dedicated his life to a single love, to a single thing so important that he was unwilling to devote any time or energy to other things. I've got a purpose in this world, too. I've got a job to do. I have to give it everything I've got. Having a partner would just take my energy away from that. I have to keep my focus on this work I'm doing.

This message to the world. This truth. This healing.

A big thing I've realized over the past few months is that we as a society have gotten so far away from the vision of the world that God intended. He gave us a roadmap, he gave us a sense of right and wrong. I'm talking about the Bible.

But we've overridden it. We've tossed that roadmap out the window because we didn't like it, and we've decided anything goes. We've decided we ought to be free. We've decided we have the right to learn more, be more, do more. We have to be open and accommodating and tolerant. Anything goes in the West. Curiosity is good, pursuit of knowledge is good. Any kind of experiment that pushes the boundaries is good!

But it isn't! Thinking like that is exactly what's causing all these problems in the first place. We're just undermining the social fabric of our society. We keep saying anything goes, anything goes. But what that means is there's no more right and wrong anymore.

That's a problem. That's a big problem. Because then people start thinking that they can do whatever they want, just because they want to. And they start doing things that they think make them look good. But so often they are things that corrupt them, hurt them, and hurt everyone else around them. They start wanting to take down the successful guys, because those guys who are successful are making them look bad. Like that guy who wrecked my racecar engine. I see it all the time in my business, too. You build a successful business, and people decide you're making them look bad, and they try to take you down.

My competitors have tried all kinds of stuff to sabotage me. They've hired staff and then sent them over to my store as a plant to learn how I do it, to learn my secret. I didn't even know it until a friend of mine told me he'd seen this employee of mine working in the optical store in the mall, too. When I confronted the kid about it, he came clean; I'll give him that, at least. But, really. Corporate espionage? In an eyewear store in Red Deer, Alberta? I mean, just do a good job and you won't have to worry about it. What sort of twisted underhand mess is that?

Other things have happened, too. They've complained to the city about where I place signs outside on the street. I place signs maybe two times a year, when we have a major frame show or something. Twice a year! And these guys go to the city council on a weekend and get them to make us remove the signs! Unbelievable. And then they try to copy my ads. Which is hilarious.

Let me tell you a little bit about my philosophy on my ads. I guess it's a philosophy on my business as a whole. I believe in always giving my customers the best value. I'm not interested in marking my product up an extra forty per cent, so I can have a forty-per-cent-off sale four times a year, when my customers get the chance to pay what they should be paying for lenses and frames. No, I give my customers the best deal I can every day. Sure, my staff's got to be paid and there are the bills, and all that. But after that, I don't need a lot of markup. I've never raised prices in ten years. My frames are the same price they have been since the day we opened. My customers are bright; they notice the difference. That's one of the reasons they come back.

Anyway, my ads are about selling me, selling my store. And they're predicated on a simple concept—always the best service, the best price, the best selection. Always. Everyday. So I don't need to promote some sale. What I do is I tell this story in my ads. They're designed to invoke a memory. It's a memory that you think of, and you think of my store, and there's a link, you see? And it works. People come in. But when the other guys try to copy it, it's hilarious! Because the whole idea undermines that sale they're trying to promote. And customers are bright. They figure it out. They notice. And they come to me. It's almost as if my competitors do my advertising for me. But they haven't figured it out yet! They think I'm the problem!

It's not just stupid local stuff like that, even. My competitors try to undercut my supply chain. I had good accounts with these guys in the States for the anti-reflective coating you can get on your lenses. It costs a bit more, buying from them, especially these days, with the loonie in the tank. Costs us a dollar thirty or more of our money just to get one American dollar. So I don't make any margin on that these days. But I've always given my customers the best, and this company was the best in the business. They'd never given me any problems. But sometimes my competitors will go to our vendors and say, "We hear you deal with Steven's business. If you keep selling to that guy, we'll take our business elsewhere." Vendors always just laugh. I do eight times the volume of anyone else close to me, so what's it going to be? My competitor's account or mine? It's not even a question.

It isn't just my competitors who try to sabotage me, either. Sometimes it's staff. Only recently I had a bookkeeper embezzle twenty thousand dollars from my business. Twenty grand! Because I had it, and she didn't, somehow she thought it was okay to take it and make it her own.

Sometimes it's even customers who sabotage. (I use the word "customers" lightly because I don't want to tarnish the names of my real customers by calling them that.) But some people will go to amazing lengths to steal product. This one lady came in with sunglasses on, and she put them up on her hat while she tried on a bunch of new pairs. And then she put her sunglasses back on the rack and put one of our pairs up on her hat. She went to the bathroom and walked out again, our glasses conveniently still on her head. Incredible.

You'd think these people would realize that stealing means we all lose. That they're feeding into something ugly by trying to build themselves up by stealing, or make themselves look better by taking me down. But they can't see that. It's as if they convince themselves that their behaviour is okay, that there isn't really such a thing as right and wrong. They tell themselves whatever they want, whatever makes them feel comfortable, whatever justifies their distorted and damaging view of the world because that's the only way they can be okay with themselves. Because they've thrown out their ability to make any kind of comparative judgment. They act as if right and wrong don't exist anymore.

That kind of stuff has been going on my whole career. My whole life. People sabotaging each other. People saying one thing and then doing something else. When I started my very first business—back when I was in my early twenties and I started a workwear business—I set up shop on the understanding that a huge gas plant that was going in nearby would buy from a local store first. That they would source gear for their crews from the nearest town. They told me as much—they specifically told me that they really wanted to buy locally, and that they wished there was a workwear store nearby that sold quality items. Because if there was, they'd do all their business there. They even told me how much they expected to spend every month.

But then, when I set up shop, they never came in. Didn't send their guys in. Maybe a few came in once or twice, but the company ordered all their stuff from Calgary and had it shipped to them. I went bankrupt in no time. It was really sad, too, because some local people kept coming in to buy things: nice, thick socks, or gloves or good coats or whatever. They told me they were trying to buy from me because they wanted me to stay. They were so happy to see a new business in town. But they were usually older ladies who were living on pensions, or people with families and tight budgets, and they just didn't have enough to spend. We all needed the company business. I'd relied on it; I'd taken a big risk because I believed their word. And I lost every penny I had. I had to declare bankruptcy. Another horrible thing to endure.

Something similar happened the next time I tried to go into business, too. It wasn't my business—I was going to join up with a woman who already had an eyewear store and wanted to expand. I was going to have shares in her business as part of joining her team. That was out in B.C, when I was working in Nelson. But it never panned out.

I don't think she lied to me outright, like the gas company. But she didn't recognize her commitments, either. She was careless with her word. And she didn't seem to think anything of it; meanwhile it landed me in a really tight spot.

It was after I'd been in Nelson for a while, and I wasn't really feeling challenged by my job anymore, working as a manager at the eyewear store in town. Anyway, I found a job posting from this woman in southern B.C. She decided she wanted someone to fit contact lenses. And she was pretty keen on me, because I had my contact lens diploma, which no one else did down there, and I was a proven manager to boot.

Anyway, I went down to her store on one of my days off, and I did an interview with her, and it went great. We got along really well, and she had strong vision for the store. I told her what I wanted for a salary, and we talked about a profit share, and agreed on terms, and everything was fine.

Lucky for me, I was thinking ahead, and I got her to put the offer in writing. That saved my bacon later. Anyway, we agreed that I would start in three weeks, because I needed to give notice to my current boss and I thought a week's vacation before I started the new job would be a nice treat. And she said fine—that sounds great.

So I went back to work and gave my notice, and I enjoyed my time off. Now, this was in March, or thereabouts, near the tail end of winter. And out of nowhere we got this terrible snowstorm. It was absolute chaos, shut the highways down and everything. I knew it was really bad, because this massive old oak tree that had stood outside my apartment forever cracked right down the middle.

I didn't think much of it initially, other than being annoyed how the storm got in the way of my vacation plans, because the roads were closed. But then, a day or two before I was due to start the new job, I called up my new boss, just to confirm that I'd be in on Monday at 9:00 a.m., like we agreed. Well, she backed out of the whole deal. She just said, "Oh, sorry. My plans have changed. The store got really damaged in that storm. And my insurance won't cover it, so I can't afford the new store. So I don't need you now. Sorry."

And that was it. No phone call to tell me, no letter, nothing. What if I'd just showed up on that Monday? And now I was stuck in Nelson with no job, no money coming in. And I didn't have money saved. I didn't even have enough money to move back home. The least she could have done would have been to call me and let me know that the job had fallen through. Then I could have gotten out of there earlier. Instead, I had to figure out a way to get out of there before the end of the month because I couldn't pay another month's rent. Eventually, I went down to the casino and did what my dad did back when he needed some cash—I bet my last forty bucks on the ponies. Well, if you'll believe it, I won eight hundred dollars. Karma at work, if I ever saw it. That was enough to get me out of there, get me moved back home, back to my parents' place in Alberta.

I didn't stay at home long. I got a job at a place in Calgary. But it wasn't a good fit; they kept doing weird stuff and trying to put me on the hook for it. And then, right around the time they parted ways with me, I hit a physical setback. I was changing a light bulb in my apartment, and I heard a pop, and my back went out. Somehow, I'd injured myself. I'd injured myself so badly that an hour later I could barely move. My whole back had seized up. I had to be helped to walk. I almost had to be carried to get around. Obviously, I couldn't work like that. I wasn't in a position to try and find another job. So I moved back to Mom and Dad's again.

Do you know how embarrassing it is to move back in with your parents when you're in your thirties? Even worse, to not be able to work? To need them to look after you? That is so debilitating. Especially when just a few months before I'd thought I was moving up in the world. That I was going to be a part-owner of a business. That I was going to be independent and set up for life.

Luckily, I have the best parents in the world. My mom introduced me to her naturopath, who was also a chiropractor. She helped me heal. It took a while, but she helped me get back on my feet. It wasn't too long before I was able to help with some small chores around my parents' house, and start moving in a healthy direction.

She was great, that woman. I knew at the time that I needed to see a chiropractor. I'd been healed by one before, by a guy in Calgary who helped me out the last time something wonky like that happened to me. But he couldn't help me this time. I tried.

See, back when I was up working in the glasses lab in northern B.C., I got this strange sort of hearing problem. Back then, I was eating healthy and trying to gain some weight. One day, I was stretching and I heard a pop in my neck. Next thing I knew my hearing was strange in one ear. It was as if I had a finger in my ear. When I talked, it felt as though I was in an airplane in half my head. Try it: Stick a finger in your ear and then talk. Nice, eh? I had this for two or three years. Went to a dozen chiropractors. I'd give them six appointments, and then move on to the next one if nothing improved.

Finally, I met a chiropractor that fixed my ear. After the fourth treatment, I remember walking out of his office back to my car and realizing, "I can hear clearly again." There was no more finger-in-my-ear feeling. It was incredible. It was totally amazing. I was healed! I was back to normal! I felt as if I was walking through a whole new world. And I was so careful when I turned my head and moved after that. I didn't want that ear problem returning.

Anyway, I'd been pretty sure all along that a chiropractor would be able to fix me. I did see a hearing specialist, too, before I got healed. A surgeon. He identified my hearing problem just fine. But he'd wanted to operate and take a biopsy of the inside of my ear. I'm glad I had enough common sense to know better, because I found someone to heal me without cutting into my body.

So, anyway, as I said, since that chiropractor had been able to heal my hearing problem, I went to the same guy to get my back fixed. But he couldn't fix it. So I was sure glad when my mom's naturopath was able to get me back to normal. It took three months of acupuncture and massage to heal me. But I got there.

The recovery process sucked. It was hard work. But one of the good things was I couldn't do much, so I spent a lot of time playing music, which was one of the few things I could still do. Man, was that a comfort to me in those times. When you're lying on your back with nothing to do, playing music and singing is the best way to ease your soul. I even had a friend in the recording business get me into his studio to record a song I wrote. It actually got played on the radio up in Edmonton a few times. That was a highlight of that time.

Eventually I found another job through a friend of mine in the optical industry—that job out in Saskatchewan. So that was good. But those few months trapped at my parents', going from a healthy young guy with a stake in a company to flat on your back at your parents' place a few months later—that took a toll.

And you can see how it fits into the larger pattern I've come to see. Everywhere, at every stage of my life, I've seen people trying to sabotage each other, people not caring about the folks around them, about the impact they have on others. It's heartbreaking. It's not what we're commanded to do. It's not how God wanted us to live. He meant for us to live in harmony, and we keep not trying. We keep turning away.

For myself, I wanted to get closer to God through Jesus Christ. I don't know how much time we have left in this world. Surely with Morgellons it can't be long. The rot of life on this planet is so obvious. We're so fallen. We've forgotten that God promised to come when we're least expecting it. I'd say we're pretty far from expecting it now. But maybe it's coming. Maybe that's what the impending planet Nibiru is all about.

And I kept thinking about Jesus. About the Holy Land. I kept thinking about the Dead Sea. About how nothing can live in it. I mean, that was the whole point of everything I'd been doing—the baking soda, the borax. I'd been trying to mimic the Dead Sea environment inside my body.

And then one day it occurred to me: Why not just go to the Dead Sea myself? If nothing can live in the Dead Sea, maybe my Morgellons couldn't live in the Dead Sea, either. Maybe going there could help cure me. It was probably a pipe dream. But at the very least it would be an environment where Morgellons couldn't live. It would be a break from Morgellons in the environment around me, and there was no way that could be bad.

And another thing: It would give me an excuse to visit Jerusalem. Travelling to the Holy Land would be such an incredible experience. Imagine how I could connect with my Lord and Saviour, Jesus Christ, if I could walk where he walked, sit where he sat, see the places he saw. Even if it brought no healing, that alone will be worth it. It would be a pilgrimage, an homage, more than just a visit to the Dead Sea.

Could I get away from the store for a trip that long? Did I even want to?

Of course I could. They could manage a week or two without me. They'd done it before. And I needed the break. I could feel my own exhaustion. I was stretched thinner than I'd ever been. I needed change. A vacation was long overdue.

I wasn't living under a rock. I knew that the Middle East was a dangerous place. But I had to go. It really wasn't an option at this point. I committed to doing whatever I had to do to beat this thing. Absolutely whatever it took. A trip to Israel couldn't do anything but good, whatever the cost.

I knew I had responsibilities to my family and to my staff. I'd have to take some care. So I looked around, did some more research online, and I found a society of Canadian Christians who take a trip to Israel every April. They go to Jerusalem and to the Dead Sea, among other places. It sounded exactly like what I'd been looking for. Plus, the timing of the trip fell neatly between pay periods. I'd be able to meet my business responsibilities, no problem. And it'd be a trip with like-minded people—Christians, believers, people who wanted to make the pilgrimage to places where Christ lived and walked and breathed.

So I booked it. I booked the trip. In the middle of April, right after Easter, I'd be going away. Going to Israel. Going to swim in the Dead Sea. I'd find hope, or a cure, or maybe both. It was going to be inspirational!

Not long after I booked the trip, I finally decided to get a dog. I hadn't had a dog in so long. I wanted a friendly face to come home to. I wanted the light in my house, the movement, the vitality.

I poked around on Kijiji, and I found an ad for a litter of Malamute Husky pups. So I went and met the guy who was selling them, and you know what his name was? Israel.

I knew then and there I had to take a pup. I mean, talk about fate. I'd just decided to take this trip to the Promised Land, and here was a man named Israel. What other sign did I need?

Well, I looked at the pups, and this one little girl caught my eye. She was all white with big blue eyes. She just tugged at my heartstrings. So I bought her and took her home. I named her Izzi, because—what else?

She brings me so much joy. She's so smart. She learns so fast. She wants to learn. She wants to make me happy. And I love playing with her. It takes my mind off things. Takes my mind off my face. Off all the horror in the world. I forget all about that, and I can just be.

I'm careful out in the yard, though. At least for now. I don't want any owl carrying her off into the night. She'll get too big for that, but for now I want to protect her. I want to keep her safe.

As I watch her play, so full of life, so full of vitality, I remember: I have something to live for. She's counting on me. And I won't let her down. I won't let anyone down.

I have a job to do. Finally, *finally*, I know why I'm here. Why I am lucky enough to be alive on this planet, at this time. I know what I'm here to do, and I will not fail. I will hold on, and I will fight, because the other way is unthinkable. I will not, cannot, betray everything I value just to get out of this present pain. No. The torment ends here. I won't take it out of this world with me. I won't give the devil that satisfaction.

I pick up the ball, and I throw it, and as the white fuzzball that is my dog tears after it, I feel life bubble up inside me, and I know I'm right. I'm going to make it. I am going to make it out alive.

Chapter 12
So Many Tears

Tears just come these days. All the time. I literally cry at everything. I didn't know there were so many ways to cry. But there are. There are tears of love. There are tears of remorse. Tears of empathy. Tears of anger and hatred. Tears of exhaustion. I've been so tired I've cried exhausted tears, only to become more tired and cry more tears! It's something else, I tell you. The tears that humans can cry when they're brought to the brink are absolutely incredible.

The smallest things bring the tears on these days: light coming through the window, the grass coming up through the ground. The other day in the store I saw this little kid helping his sister, and I felt tears well up at the joy of it, at the simple humanity of it. I thought, *Yeah, little buddy. You've got it, you've got that heart. Hang on to it, man!*

I feel like the biggest cry baby. I'm a leaky faucet. My eyes just run and run and run. But I can't help it. And I wouldn't, even if I could. These tears are proof that I care. They're proof that I'm alive, that I have a heart, that I have a soul. Nothing is more valuable than that. After all I've been through, I can definitively say, nothing is more important that growing your heart, than touching your soul.

We're put here to love. Plain and simple. We're put here to love each other, to love our planet, to love God. He gave us his only son, didn't he? He gave us the most precious thing he could imagine. He gave up a divine life to come here and be with us and teach us about the nature of love.

I just want to share that with you. That love, that thankfulness. I know we can't do anything to halt the rotting of this planet. I know it's too late. We can't undo the damage on a global scale. But each of us can save ourselves. We can choose something different. We can choose something human. We can choose connection. And connection comes from love and from faith and from thankfulness.

Like I said at the start, I am so thankful for the choices I've made. For the business I've built that has given me the opportunity to face this thing. That I haven't had to go in, nine-to-five every day, after I've been up working on my face until 4:00 a.m. Because I've had the freedom to live and to heal, I've been able to learn and grow and share. I am so thankful to all my employees for that. For making that possible. For making it possible for me to live out my purpose.

I'm so thankful that I've had the opportunity to write this book. To step back and look at the whole of my life, and say: Wow. I am one lucky guy. Look at all the amazing things I've done in my life. That I've had the opportunity to do! Look at how they've led me to this place where I can take on this incredible, impossible challenge. And I can dig in and find a way.

I'm so thankful for my best friend, for the life-changing surgery he made it through. He had a brain tumor the size of a fist successfully removed, and even though he's plagued by headaches every day, he's still there for me as I go through all of this. I'm so thankful for my nephew—his help and support make it possible for me to continue. Even in the darkest days of his life, he understands Uncle Steven. And I'm so thankful to my mom. That she's still here with me at eighty years old, still healthy and supportive at every turn. I'm thankful for my dad, and my grandmas and my grandpas on the other side, for the spiritual strength they've lent me.

I want people to know—people who are suffering—take comfort. It won't be long now. Christ will come, and he will lift us up, just as he promised. I promise, it will happen. Real soon.

I want all of you who've tried to hurt me, to know: You tried to destroy me. You made my life a living hell. You did everything you could. You tried to shatter my being; you tried to take away all the things I love. Well, you've just made me stronger. I can live through whatever you throw at me. Even as I've watched, you've destroyed yourselves and your world in an effort to take me down. But it hasn't worked. It hasn't worked. I've got Christ on my side. I've got love in my heart. I am full of love and empathy and tears, and grief doesn't even matter anymore. All that's left is forgiveness and gratitude.

If you've made it this far, read this far into my book, let a little of my life into your world and into your heart—thank you. Thanks for helping me to fulfil my mission. I couldn't have done it without you. What I ask now is go out and live. Really live. Connect with other people. Put down your phones, come out from behind your computer screens, and remember what it's like to be human. Reach out to the humans around you. Reach out to yourself. Be alone, truly alone. Reach out to God through Jesus Christ. Let the spirit move you. Let love in. That's all you need to do. Reach out. Connect. Be human. That's how you find your purpose. That's how you change the world.

Inside myself I can feel the winter ending. Inside myself I can feel change. Things are shifting. My whole life is shifting. I've changed. I live through each agonizing day, and I find a way to smile.

The year turns, and I turn with it. It's Easter. The season of renewal.

I have never before understood the concept of sacrifice so clearly. I have never understood the agony of unraveling before. I have been brought to my knees. I am broken and crying and sniveling in the dirt, and I am not worthy.

But I have been lifted up. I have been seen and loved and cherished. I have been blessed by my Lord and Saviour, Jesus Christ. I have never been so grateful for and so dependent on the love of another. Without him, I would be nothing, but with him, I am so, so much. I am one of his sacred children. I am alive and living and loving in him.

When you come through the darkness that I've been through, when you see the destruction of mankind and the world and everything you loved like I have, when you see how few people on this planet actually give a damn about the fate of humanity, or the environment, or even their own family, when you see so many people unable to give a damn about anything but themselves—and then experience the holy and transformative love of the Saviour for no reason other than because you *are* and because you *believe*, you *see* him and cling to him in your agony. And to find that that witnessing—that witnessing of Christ, of something whole and pure and good and so much bigger than yourself—is so big, so *so* big, and to discover that just acknowledging him, honouring him brings so much love, and to think that he loves *me*, little, broken, messed-up Steven Petersen...my God, it's heartbreaking.

It's so beautiful that it's heartbreaking.

I have never felt so blessed and so small and so beloved in my whole entire life. This year, I finally got the concept of grace. Of mercy. Of love.

And let me tell you, I could never have made it through the last ten months without him. Because I am not alone. My Lord and Saviour, Jesus Christ, walks with me every minute of every day. Because I walk with him. I put my faith in him. I fix my mind on him. I think about him, every single minute of every single day. There's not a moment that goes by where I'm not in prayer. In this special place of love and light and connection far removed from this physical earth.

You know, the other day—night, I should say; it was late—I'd been praying all day, literally all day long. And it was three in the morning and I had to go and take some cheques to the bank, and I went out and sat in my car, and it was like I was in a dream. And I kept slapping my knee, saying, "Wake up, Steve. Wake up." Slap. "Steven. Wake up." Slap. "You need to come back to this world, Steven. You need to come back." Slap. "I need you here now, Steve." Slap, slap. And it really was like that. Like I was calling myself back from somewhere else. Someplace where I'd been communing with God. I'd meditated so far into whatever spiritual realm he was in, that I had to call myself back to earth, had to remind myself that this is the physical world I live in. That's how close I feel to God these days. That's how much I rely on Jesus Christ, on his spiritual love, on that connection with him.

It's a pretty powerful reminder that this isn't only a physical plane. That we aren't only physical beings. That we live in a spiritual plane as well as a physical one. And we ought to remember that. We can remember it, no matter where we are or what we've done. I mean, look at my life. I'm no saint. I've done a lot of stupid things. Hurtful things. But I'm still loved. I can still open that spiritual door. I don't even have to open it; it's always been there. Just waiting for me to see it. Waiting for me to want it. And Christ was always on the other side, waiting for me. Loving me.

God, I sound like such a pouf. Like all those blathering TV evangelists. Like all those people who proclaim their faith for some shallow reason. Because they want attention, or because they think it's what they should say. I hate people like that. I hate being lumped in with them. I hate that I will be lumped in with them, because people can't see.

But that's just my pride talking. It doesn't matter what they think, or what you think, or what anyone thinks. What matters is that I know that I am loved. That God loves me. That he gave up his son for me. That Christ died for *me*. And that as I live through this chaos, I am living my destiny on this planet.

All my pain is a testament to how much I love my God. It's reminded me that there's a God to love! And if that doesn't make me grateful, nothing will. Nothing could. I mean, I am filled with so much thankfulness it knocks the wind out of me. I just start weeping, streaming tears for no reason, other than God has given me this purpose, to walk out in the world and live this truth. And that's the most valuable gift he could ever give anyone. And he's given it to me.

He is risen.

I am so blessed.

That love I felt from Easter—that place of deep revelation, of uplifting spirit—haunted me until I got on the plane for Israel. Until I was lifted into the sky, heading toward the Promised Land. I was going to walk where he walked. Touch things he touched. I will be closer to my Lord and Saviour, Jesus Christ, than I've ever been. At least on this physical plane.

I wasn't travelling alone. There were a bunch of other people on the tour.

We were a strange mix, we Canadians. We came from all over the country, from all walks of life. We all had our own reasons for crossing the world and going back to our spiritual birthplace. We didn't talk about it too much, amazingly. We just enjoyed that we all cared. Because we had this in common: we love our Lord and Saviour, and we wanted to walk where he walked. We all knew it to be desperately important. We all knew it would change us somehow.

There was one guy in particular who really impressed me. He knows Jesus, really knows him. It's in his eyes. The way he looks at the world, the way he greets other people, the way he honours them and loves them for just being alive and loving God. It's amazing. His eyes are so intense. I don't think I'll ever forget them. They're such a gift. Whenever I get in one of my funks—feeling down and low and suicidal—I'll just think of him. I'll think of him and the way his eyes look at the world, and I remember: I am one of God's chosen children, and I am loved.

My time in Jerusalem was mind-blowing. Every day of my trip was packed full, from beginning to end. I didn't even have time to worry about my face, to spend time caring for it. Instead, I was out in the world, breathing in the magic of the Holy Land.

Seeing the Wailing Wall, where folks from so many walks of life come to pray for the world, was really something. I was really struck by the way the old Jews bob and wail before that wall. They are so full of grief! It's as if they are in mourning. Don't they know God is alive? That Jesus triumphed over the pain of this life? Why do they still grieve for him? I wish they'd stop living in mourning and shame and embrace the eternal love of the Lord. I just wanted to open up to them about the glory that lives in this moment! In each and every one of them!

I kept wanting to offer myself, my faith, my spiritual energy. But I was afraid to. I was afraid of being rebuffed. I was afraid of offending someone. For example, there was this one woman sitting in the street, her infant child beside her on a blanket. She was begging for alms to heal her sick child. I wanted to kneel on the blanket with them. I wanted to offer to pray, to lay my hands on her child and pray for it. But I didn't. I didn't know if she would understand me. I didn't know if she would trust I acted in the good faith of Christ.

So I didn't. I walked on past. Later, at the hotel, I saw two older gentle-men—Orthodox Jews—outside the door. One of them was older than I am, probably by about ten years; I'd say he was sixty or so. The other one was older even than that. They might have been father and son. Anyway, I wanted to take a picture of them. I went up to one of them—the younger one—and I asked, "Could I have your picture?" He looked at me a minute, then he said something in Hebrew to the older man. The older man replied, just a couple of words. The younger one pondered it for a while more, then he looked at me and shook his head. "No." He wasn't rude about it. He just said it simply and firmly: "No."

I was glad I'd asked. And in that moment I absolved myself of any anxiety I'd had—about not speaking of my joy in the living Lord, of not praying with the mother and the baby, and a million other things. In refusing a simple picture, that one man had shown me that it was just as well. I was glad I didn't offer to wash their feet instead; I would have had to touch them, and they would not have heard or understood me anyway. They're a people with their heads stuck in the past; they have no time for the living future.

One of the most amazing experiences of the whole trip was a visit to a church with incredible acoustics. The whole sanctuary echoed and echoed with every sound you made. It has a resonance of eight seconds.

The whole group of us sang in that space. We wanted to feel the workings of God in the music, in that incredible space built in his honour.

We sang "Amazing Grace." How fitting is that? That's why we were all there, in one way or another, to witness his grace. And we all knew it.

We sang it slowly, one small phrase at a time.

"Ama-zing Grace—"pause "—How sweet the sound—"pause "—that saved a wretch—" pause "—like me…"

And every time we paused, we'd just stand there in awe, listening to the echoes ring and ring, hearing the harmonies brought to life in the music, just hanging in the air, glorifying God. I tell you, I've never heard anything so beautiful.

When we got to the end of the first verse, not everyone knew the rest, so we just sang, "Praise God—Praise God—Praise God—Praise God!" To the same tune as "Amazing Grace," but just with those words. Because it was so beautiful, we just couldn't stop. I sank to my knees in tears there in that hall, singing and weeping and just giving my love to the Lord. I'll never forget it. What a moment. What a memory.

Finally we got to the Dead Sea. The Dead Sea—ah, the Dead Sea. It's the lowest point on earth—four hundred and seventeen feet below sea level. It truly is like no place else. I'd been thinking of it and imagining it and putting so much hope in it, thinking of the chance to bathe in its wondrous properties, soak in its salty cure. And when we got off the bus I waited only long enough for a moment of prayer and reflection. Then I plunged right in.

You really do float. The water held me up so well, I couldn't get my feet under. I was out there, swimming around in the Dead Sea—or as much as you can swim in it. It's really more like scooting. I'd scoot across the surface like a water bug. No matter how hard I'd try, I could not get my feet to stay under the water. Our guide laughed and laughed at me. "In all the years I've been doing this, I've never seen someone who couldn't get his feet wet!" he said. The sand there is something else, too. It's like mud, only pliable almost. Like clay, I guess. It is so soft and smooth and cool—I took some and I smeared it all over my body.

While I was out there swimming, I kept plunging my hands down into the clay below the water, digging for rocks. You've got to be careful, digging for rocks. The minerals congeal into these hard little pebbles. But if you crush the mineral bits between your fingers, the minerals crumble. The rocks don't. So I plunged my hands into the seabed until I felt what seemed like a rock. Then I'd bring it up and crush it, just to be sure. And if it actually was a rock, I'd slip it into my pocket. I kept doing that all afternoon. By the time we got back on the bus, I had twelve. My favourite number. Neat, eh?

I rode all the way back to our hotel in my swim trunks. Everyone else brought a change of clothes, but I wanted to keep that water close to my skin as long as I possibly could. So I sat on the bus in my wet shorts all the way back. It was pretty warm, so it wasn't really uncomfortable. When we got back to the hotel, I took my shorts off and hung them up, and the next day, they were stiff and solid, as if they'd been starched. I stood them up on the floor.

On one of our last days, we went to the Sea of Galilee, which is the site of one of Jesus's most unbelievable and effortless miracles. It is where he walked on water. His disciples were out in a boat. They'd left him on shore, and he walked out to them, even in the midst of a storm.

We all got to go out in a boat, out onto the Sea of Galilee. It's absolutely beautiful—wide clear water as far as the eye can see. It's quite shallow a long way out, but we were out far enough that it was pretty deep. Anyway, we were sitting in the cabin of this fishing boat, talking, and suddenly I realized: We're in the middle of the Sea of Galilee. What are we all doing sitting inside?

I wanted to be outside, looking at this place. So I got up quietly, and I went out onto the deck.

I was the only person out there. I walked to the prow of the boat, and I just stood there looking out at the water. And I had this feeling inside me that everything is going to be okay. Just a feeling of peace. A feeling like when you notice the water going down after a flood—just relief and joy and gratitude.

I took my shirt off and looked at my skin, and I saw that the lesions were healing. My skin looked better than it has in months. A year, maybe. It looked *good*. And it came to me, then, that I am healing. God has brought me through hell, and brought me to this place of deliverance, and I have been changed. I am healing. My body is purging this menace, and I will be free.

I climbed up onto the prow and stood there, gazing out over the waters of Galilee, and I lifted up my arms and I prayed—in gratitude, in thanksgiving. I wept tears of joy and relief and love, and I thanked Jesus and God for bringing me here, for bringing me through.

And as I sat there, praying my gratitude and my acknowledgement and my awareness of him, thanking him for my purpose—it started to rain.

Soft gentle rain on my skin, a blessing from heaven.

Epilogue

I wish I could say everything was rosy and perfect when I got home. That all this mess and this disease just miraculously sorted themselves out. But I can't. This is not a fairy tale. It's not fiction. It's life. And life is messy.

The first few weeks at home were full of hope. Hope and change and health. But it didn't take long for omens to show that all was not well. I started getting the sores again. And other ugly reminders lifted their heads up, too.

I had a court case, not long after I was back—this guy I'd hired to do some work on my house was taking me to court because I hadn't paid him. Course, he'd done such a shoddy job that I was worse off than when he started, and I'd refused to pay him, which is why he was taking me to court. But I was all prepared—I had photos of the "work," and estimates of the damage done, and the costs I'd have to lay out to get the work redone, and all that. But what do you think happened? The judge got up in front of the courtroom before we even began, and he said, "Gentlemen, I want to be absolutely clear about one thing. This court does not care about what is right or just, in cases like this. What this court cares about is money. So I would like to ask you whether you might want to take a few minutes and consider a settlement before we get going. I'm going to step out. I'll be back in ten minutes. See if you can't work something out."

Well, that was a familiar song. I shouldn't have been surprised. And I realized that what I wanted—the right course of action, someone taking responsibility for their mistakes and paying for them—was not going to be honoured in that courtroom. And so I settled. I figured that I'd have to pay some money one way or another, and I'd just as soon have the whole thing over with. So I offered the guy forty per cent of what I owed him, and he agreed. When the judge came back in, we said, "Thanks, but we don't need you anymore." And I left.

But it was stressful. Another reminder of the corrupt material world. Even our courts are infested. When the judge openly admits he doesn't care about what is right, that he only cares about money—the best thing I could do was step away. I should've known better than to expect justice in this life. It's only when we leave this life that we'll get true justice in God.

Anyway, after that court case, and after my sores opened up again, I started looking for an exfoliant. I had this feeling that if I could find something to help me scrub the sand out of my skin, I'd speed up the healing process. So anyway, I tried a bunch of things, starting with an old apricot exfoliant I used to like. But it wasn't really helping, just irritating my skin. And then one day, as I was preparing my borax wash, I saw the tiny little grains of borax, the borax dust, and I thought, why not? I keep diluting this stuff to use it on my body, why not just use it like this? So I got my skin just a little bit moist, and I got a bunch of the borax in my hands, and I just rubbed it straight onto my skin.

Well, it was like the first time I ever did a borax wash. So much grit just came right out of my skin. It was so revealing. Here I'd been thinking I was beating this thing, and there was still so much of it in my skin! This method is the only one I use, now. I don't bother with the borax wash anymore. I just rub the borax powder straight onto my skin. And it works.

I take baths, too. I pour a whole box of borax or baking soda into the tub and I soak in it. At first, when I got home, I was trying to replicate my day in the Dead Sea, and I'd stay in the tub for hours and hours: four hours, six hours, eight hours, even. But it wasn't long before I realized the tub water was taking on a really weird colour. It would get milky. And not from the borax, or the baking soda—there wasn't enough of it to turn the whole tub milky like that. No, it was after I'd been sitting in it for half an hour or an hour that it'd turn like that.

I started draining the tub as soon as I noticed it, and the bottom was all filled with this slimy goo, and I rinsed it all out and filled it again, and soaked in it again, and after a while the same thing happened. And finally I realized what it was. The Morgellons fibres that are coming out of my skin, that the borax is drawing out, aren't really killed. They might be drawn out of my body, but that doesn't incapacitate them. Remember, nothing on earth — *nothing* — can kill Morgellons. So I figured they were starting to reform in the water. And let me tell you, I do not want those bits anywhere near my skin. I spend so much time and effort getting them out of my body, I don't want to give them any chance to get back in. So now I don't soak in the tub for more than half an hour without replacing the water.

Speaking of the bits reforming, I've noticed something else. The fibres are starting to form together underneath my skin. It's as if they've got little tails on them. I can trace these long, hard, wiry threads underneath my skin, stretching out from one lesion in all directions. Sometimes, they even join one lesion up with another. They're making a literal web in my skin.

I can trace the wires with my fingers. Sometimes, if they feel close enough to the surface, I scrape them out. You can see them: little white bits of stuff, like metal. I scrape them out with my thumbnail most times. Sometimes I need to use a little nail file, or a pair of tweezers. But I've got to get them out. I don't want this stuff in my body. Building up. Assembling.

It's starting to stretch down my arms now. I have sores on my left hand, in between my fingers. And the wiry, webby stuff twists down my forearm and joins up with it. And man, does it hurt. It hurts way worse than any of the ones on my face do.

I've got sores on my thighs now, too. And a couple on my abdomen. It's spreading, this thing. It's taking over my body little by little. I sure haven't beaten it yet. That confidence I had coming home from Jerusalem seems so naive now.

I don't know where this thing is going. I don't know what it's going to take to heal me. I know I'm on the right path. I see the evidence of it, in the grit I find in the tub, in the wires I tear out from under my skin. But I can't predict the course this thing will take. I might heal all the way. It might take two months, it might take two years. I don't know. I don't know if I'll be bed-ridden. I don't know if I'll ever be healed.

The truth is I don't even care anymore. What happens to my body is irrelevant. It's not that I can live through it easily—I can't. I still struggle every day with the mess and the pain and the fear of what comes next. But I've finally accepted the disease. I accept that it is what it is, and it's going to do what it's going to do to my body. I fight it with the tools I have—the borax exfoliant, the bracelets, the baking soda. I fight back physically. It's part of my moral duty. But I have accepted that whatever is going to happen to my body is going to happen. The reason I'm able to accept it is that I have won the battle for my soul.

That's what going to Israel really did for me. It saved my soul. I have gotten past the worst of the battle. I know whose side I'm on now. I know that, even if I physically rebel, or mentally rebel, I will survive. Because my soul is clean. It's been healed. Being in the Holy Land, following God's call to fight this thing—these things have cleansed me, have saved my soul.

The day-to-day of my life is different now.

My nephew has moved in with me. He's an alcoholic. He has been forever. But he's finally coming out of it. He knows he has to. He's on his last chance. He had a run of forty days dry then he fell off the wagon again. The doctors are amazed that he lived, said he doesn't have another bounce-back in him. His body literally can't take it. If he binges again, he'll die. Anyway, he didn't have anywhere to go, really, and I could see he needed something to live for. So he lives with me now, and we look out for each other. I keep him sober; he keeps me sane. It's such a relief, not to be the only person alone in the house. After I've been up until the middle of the night, into the early morning, even, working on my skin, it's such a gift to have someone to talk to. And I get to share what I've learned in my life—about the I Ching, about listening to the world, about loving God. And he's all I've got. I'm all he's got. We have each other's backs. And it works. He's been sober for a couple of months now.

Another big change: I've sold my business. Made my money on it. An old colleague of mine who stepped in to help me back in the spring, when I just needed to take a break from the day-to-day, well, he was in a position to buy me out. And it felt right. So I sold it. I've moved on.

I feel free.

And it isn't just because I've closed a chapter of my life. The biggest thing is, since I've been home, I've fully realized that it just isn't possible for people to acknowledge this whole Morgellons mess. It's so beyond their language. They can hear a tiny piece of what I'm saying—like, maybe they can grasp that there's something there. But that's it. They just don't have the ability to make sense of this story. It's beyond their capacity. And I'm okay with that. I've accepted it. Because I see how far I've come and what the cost of that has been, and I know that most people will never get there, let alone imagine that such a journey is humanly possible.

Let's be honest. Most people can't even acknowledge that God or Christ exists anymore. Even though they acknowledge it implicitly all the time. I mean, every time we write the date, we mean it's two thousand plus years after Christ came and died. I mean, that's implied. But people forget. Or they ignore it. And if they forget or ignore something as simple as that, nothing I ever say is going to convince them to think of things differently.

But that's okay. I'm not here to do that. I'm not here to save the world, change the world, fix the world, fix your soul, save you. I'm just here to tell you about me and my life. And how Steven came to figure this all out.

And the answer is simple. It's because I paid attention. I wasn't too preoccupied with all these other things that don't really matter. But I have been in touch with what does matter: I matter. My soul matters. My spirit matters.

And knowing that, it was easy to pay attention to all the different things. To stare at the sky at night, to see the sky during the day, to see the birds, to see the trees, to see all these connections between things. To see it all, and then see it get ugly, uglier and uglier. But you don't realize how ugly things are when that's all you know.

I was here to uncover this. Uncover my life. To tell you how I saved my life. And how I knew to. Simply just by living it. But always holding on to that sense of spirit and soul that dwells within me. I'm just here to tell you that. And maybe, just maybe, there's a spark inside of you that recognizes something in my story. And through me sharing my story with you, maybe you can do something for yourself. And if not, we'll all carry on in our own way.

But if anything should come of this, it's going to be on an individual level, a personal level. Because I can't fix the world. But maybe you will stand the chance when you hear this. When you hear about my life, maybe you will know what I know. Believe what I believe. That my life is worth knowing, worth saving, and yours is, too.

So when you have that chance, take it. Even if it's cloaked in misery and discomfort, even if it seems impossible and horrible and like your worst nightmare—worse than your worst nightmare—take the chance. Open your mind, open your heart, open your eyes. See and know and believe in your own life, and watch God at work, witness miracles happen.

Because it truly is possible in his mercy.

Amen.

Resources

Books

The Cure for All Diseases: With Many Case Histories. Hulda Regehr Clark. Ph.D.,N.D. New Century Press, Chula Vista, 1995.

The Tao of I Ching: Way to Divination. Jou, Tsung Hwa. Tai Chi Foundation, Taiwan, 1984.

Websites

1) Morgellons Cure : http://morgellonscure.com/

2) Morgellons Research : http://www.morgellons-research.org/

3) Morgellons.ca : http://morgellons.ca/

YouTube Videos

General Background Videos

1) Morgellons Disease - Nano Genocide - Environmental Warfare
   https://www.youtube.com/watch?v=C4oNn1rSq3A

2) From Chemtrails to Pseudo-Life:
   The Dark Agenda of Synthetic Biology
   https://www.youtube.com/watch?v=JfgGzLZBIU0

3) From ChemTrails to Pseudo-Life Part 2
   https://www.youtube.com/watch?v=18IepieChOU

Harald Kautz-Vella Videos
https://www.youtube.com/watch?v=j88BcgzzcTc

https://www.youtube.com/watch?v=HtAQdxowpYA

https://www.youtube.com/watch?v=eKctLpxGbsE

https://www.youtube.com/watch?v=R7VpXCoBpTs

Thank you to Kristin Fast for ghostwriting this book for me, and to TellWell Publishing for making it possible to share in the world.

CPSIA information can be obtained
at www.ICGtesting.com
Printed in the USA
LVOW11s0834171216
517043LV00001BA/4/P

9 781773 024967